1939-1945
WORLD WAR TWO

D1224877

AUTHOR

Francesco Mattesini, *born in Arezzo (Italy) on April 14, 1936. He moved to Rome in July 1951 and he served, as civilian employee, at the Italian Army General Staff, 4th Department, from 1959 to 2000. Collaborator of the Historical Offices of the Italian Military Navy and the Air Force Historical Office, for which 20 books and about 60 essays were produced. He is currently retired, always living in Rome.*

PUBLISHING'S NOTES

None of unpublished images or text of our book may be reproduced in any format without the expressed written permission of Luca Cristini Editore (already Soldiershop.com) when not indicate as marked with license creative commons 3.0 or 4.0. Luca Cristini Editore has made every reasonable effort to locate, contact and acknowledge rights holders and to correctly apply terms and conditions to Content.

Every effort has been made to trace the copyright of all the photographs. If there are unintentional omissions, please contact the publisher in writing at: info@soldiershop.com, who will correct all subsequent editions.

Our trademark: Luca Cristini Editore©, and the names of our series & brand: Soldiershop, Witness to war, Museum book, Bookmoon, Soldiers&Weapons, Battlefield, War in colour, Historical Biographies, Darwin's view, Fabula, Altrastoria, Italia Storica Ebook, Witness To History, Soldiers, Weapons & Uniforms, Storia etc. are herein © by Luca Cristini Editore.

LICENSES COMMONS

This book may utilize part of material marked with license creative commons 3.0 or 4.0 (CC BY 4.0), (CC BY-ND 4.0), (CC BY-SA 4.0) or (CC0 1.0). We give appropriate attribution credit and indicate if change were made in the acknowledgments field. Our WTW books series utilize only fonts licensed under the SIL Open Font License or other free use license.

For a complete list of Soldiershop titles please contact Luca Cristini Editore on our website: www.soldiershop.com or www.cristinieditore.com. E-mail: info@soldiershop.com

Titolo: **OPERATION "MINCEMEAT"** Code.: **WTW-045 EN** by Francesco Mattesini.
ISBN code: 978-88-93279864 first edition June 2023
Language: English. Size: 177,8x254mm. Cover & Art Design: Luca S. Cristini

WITNESS TO WAR (SOLDIERSHOP) is a mark of Luca Cristini Editore, via Orio, 33/D - 24050 Zanica (BG) ITALY.

1939-1945
WORLD WAR TWO

WITNESS TO WAR

OPERATION "MINCEMEAT"
THE MAN WHO NEVER WAS AND THE STAGING THAT DID NOT FOOL THE GERMANS

PHOTOS & IMAGES FROM WORLD WARTIME ARCHIVES

FRANCESCO MATTESINI

SOLDIERSHOP PUBLISHING

BOOKS TO COLLECT

CONTENTS

▲ A scene from the 1956 film 'The Man Who Never Was'. The corpse has the briefcase containing the fake documents and personal effects attached to his wrist with a chain.

INTRODUCTION

AUTHOR'S CONSIDERATIONS

The idea to write this book came to me after watching the Italian TV show *Tagadà* (Channel 7) aired on the afternoon of 11 November 2021. In it, there was a long reconstruction of a famous episode, which would have been decisive in facilitating the landing of the Anglo-Americans in Sicily on 10 July 1943, because it would have put the Italian and especially the German commands in the belief that the landing would take place in Greece or Sardinia. Nothing could be more inaccurate. It is regrettable that, having put the Germans in the conviction that there would be no landing in Sicily, was commented on by one of the presenters of the programme as: '***Fortunately***'.

At this point I felt offended and immediately posted the following in the AIDMEN (Italian Association of Maritime Documentation) forum: But, '*Do these gentlemen know that at that time the Italians were fighting for the defence of the homeland and that there were thousands of dead*'. This was followed by an essay posted on my *academia.edu* page, referring, for the title, to the famous 1956 British film '*The Man Who Never Was*', which was followed in 2022, after 55 years, by a new film on the same subject, with the title *Operation Mincemeat*.

I believe that the belief in the German enemy and invader even when he was a loyal ally, who for three years allowed poor and poorly defended monarchical Italy, with a fascist government, not to collapse under the British attack, derives from the fact that politicians ignorant of History, if not prejudiced, have found disciples, particularly in the political field, equally ignorant of History, claiming that '*the liberation of Italy began in Sicily*'. That is, fifteen days before 25 July 1943 and the fall of Benito Mussolini and Fascism, and almost two months after the signing of the armistice, and then the '*unconditional*' surrender of Cassibile and the subsequent declaration of 8 September. In it, the news was announced over the radio that Italy had signed the armistice, whose unilateral conditions imposed by the Allies were not known, because they were kept secret within the Court, by the Head of Government, Marshal Pietro Badoglio, and by General Vittorio Ambrosio, Head of the *Supreme Command*.

And from the armistice the national disaster began, because in addition to two opposing foreign armies fighting fiercely on the peninsula, the Anglo-Americans to conquer the land to approach Germany's borders, the Germans to prevent it, there was the unfortunate civil war that led to thousands of deaths on both sides in the conflict, fascists and anti-fascists, for ideological and power reasons.

The signing of the armistice, in fact, did not imply for the Anglo-Americans to accept Italy as an ally, but only as a co-belligerent, and therefore, an ambiguous formula, in which Italy remained for the Anglo-Americans still an enemy, but with the clause that its conduct in the war against Germany in aid of the United Nations would eventually be decisive in obtaining some facilitation. This aid, at least in the form requested by the Allies during the armistice talks and agreements that led General Giuseppe Castellano to sign on 3 September 1943 in Cassibile (Sicily), on behalf of the Head of the Italian Government, and with the decisive authorisation of the Italian King, Victor Emmanuel III, was very modest; starting immediately with the non-defence of Rome and the failure to support the Allied landing at Salerno, which was supposed to take place under the cover of the Italian Armed Forces, and which failed completely, angering the Anglo-Americans, who remained bogged down in that area of Campania, due to the prompt German reaction, until the end of September 1943, and the arrival in Rome, which was supposed to take place within a week, occurred on 4 June 1944. And Italy paid the consequences.

The signing of the peace treaty in Paris in 1947, by the Head of Government, the Honourable Alcide De Gasperi, led to particularly punitive treatment for the nation, with the loss of the colonies and part of the national territory and the surrender of units of the fleet, the reduction to a minimum of the Armed Forces as had been demanded and obtained by Russia, France, Greece and Yugoslavia, who had been the true allies of the Anglo-Americans. They demanded and obtained for the Italians, the invaders of their nations, the harshest punishment, which had already begun with the indiscriminate massacres at the foibe by Marshal Tito's communist acolytes, towards the Italian populations of Istria and Dalmatia, finally forced to exodus from their homes, welcomed into the Mother Country by the Italian communists with hatred and harassment.

For the Allies (who after the landings at Salerno, Taranto and Bari, in September 1943, behaved in the peninsula as absolute masters, assuming full powers everywhere and practically imposing the disarmament of what remained of the Royal Armed Forces, in large part by ceding arms to the French of General De Gaulle), the Italian campaign had not been a war of liberation, as it is flaunted in Italy, in television broadcasts. It was merely a strategic conquest of territory defended palm to palm by the Germans, which cost the Anglo-Americans a huge military and logistical effort and thousands of dead, and with the civil war between Italians a tragedy within a tragedy.

The Allies ended up cursing the day in mid-August 1943 when Castellano presented himself in Lisbon to their representatives to ask for an armistice, and their support in fighting the Germans, on the grounds that since they were now considered the invaders of Italy, the Italian Armed Forces also wanted to contribute to it. This behaviour of Italy is still considered a petty betrayal in Germany, which was made even more bitter by the King's escape from Rome, with the approval, although never proven, of an agreement with Field Marshal Albert Kesselring, Commander of the German forces in central and southern Italy[1] .

The war in Italy ended on 28 April 1945 with the indisputable victory of the Allies, and in it the partisan formations had little importance, except for a few acts of sabotage, harshly repressed in reprisal by the Germans at the expense of the civilian population. Better was the support provided by the Royal Armed Forces, in particular by the Combat Groups, made up of an infantry brigade, which, however, were not autonomous because they were framed in the British and Polish Divisions, which exercised command and provided the support of tanks and heavy artillery, not supplied by the Allies to the Italians.

The flaunted anti-fascism is still today a divisive element, of hatred and not of pacification, among Italians, and it would be desirable not to hear about it any more, leaving the task of describing it only to the intelligence and seriousness of non-politicised historians, as was initiated many years ago, albeit with some understandable caution, by Professor Renzo De Felice.

If Italy, like Germany and Japan, survived the disaster, and the three nations did not find themselves in the condition of Germany at the end of the First World War that later led to Nazism, this was only due to the generosity of the Americans, and the aid of their Marshall Plan that led our nation to the Economic Miracle of the 1950s-1960s.

FRANCESCO MATTESINI

▲ US General Dwight David Eisenhower, Commander-in-Chief of the Allied Forces, then post-war Commander of NATO and then President of the United States of America.

1 Francesco Mattesini, *La Marina e l'8 settembre, I Tomo, 'Le ultime operazioni offensive della Regia Marina e il dramma della Forza Navale da Battaglia'*; Ufficio Storico della Marina Militare, Rome, 2002. Francesco Mattesini, *8 September 1943. Dall'armistizio al mito della difesa di Porta San Paolo*, RiStampa Edizioni, Santa Ruffina di Cittaducale (RI), April 2021.

CHAPTER 1

THE PLANNING OF THE 'MINCEMEAT'OPERATION
AND ITS IMPLEMENTATION

In the run-up to the landings in Sicily in the spring and summer of 1943, code-named Operation 'Husky', the Anglo-American commandos, under the command of US General Dwight David Eisenhower, put in place very elaborate measures to confuse the enemy about the date and destination of the attack. Among other things, in the hope of delaying reinforcements to Sicily, to reduce the air threat to their invasion convoys and to keep the main naval forces, battleships and cruisers, away from the area of Sicily, false information was artfully provided through agents in neutral nations, such as Portugal and Spain.

Operation 'Mincemeat' was part of a main deception plan, of a much more complex operation, called 'Barkley', planned by the British, to deceive the Germans about their real landing target, Sicily.

General Eisenhower reported in one of his memoirs that preparations for Operation 'Husky', the landing in Sicily, had begun in his Algiers Command in February 1943, and its implementation, after the conclusion of the African campaign, was to take place in early July. But there was concern about the defence that would be offered by Italian and German troops, which Eisenhower explained as follows[2] :

"Experience had taught us that we did not have to fear the resistance of the Italian formations too much; however, in this operation they had to defend their territory, which could change the situation a lot. The leaders of our Information Service were deeply concerned about the strength of the German garrison. We thought - and later experience proved us right - that the German garrison at the time of the attack was substantially larger than two fully armed and equipped divisions, the assault we were planning would be too weak, and it would be reasonable to postpone the operation until we could make a greater concentration of our forces".

In Operation Barkley, as Klaus-Jurgen Muller, professor of modern and contemporary history at the Bundeswehr University and Hamburg State University, wrote in 1987, Operation 'Mincemeat' is not mentioned, and was only a deceptively fictitious addition to the 'Barkley' plan, the purpose of which was to convince the Germans that the Allies could attack Corsica, Sardinia or Greece rather than Sicily. The Germans had to believe that the conquest of Corsica and Sardinia, to be carried out with General George Patton's US army, would give the Allies a base for a potential attack on Rome or even further north around Livorno or Genoa, or in the south of France. The invasion of Greece, through the use of an imaginary British 12ª Army of twelve divisions under the command of General Harold Alexander, to which was added another fictitious concentration of troops in Cyrenaica (Operation Wartfall). could convince Turkey to enter the war with the Allies, and then allow, with Turkish support, an advance into the Balkans, in the direction of Bulgaria. The ultimate goal was to make people believe in a reunion with the Soviets and to start a co-operation with them, which was a threat particularly feared by Germany.

To make Barkley's fictitious plan more credible, to be considered by the Germans to be imminently realised, false troop movements were to be added, numerous beach raids, transmissions to Greek elements, the broadcasting of false information, radio transmissions, and the handing over of maps of the Greek coastline. Operation 'Animals' was also organised, which took place between 21 June and 11 July, in collaboration with the SOE (Special Operations Executive), and US Air Force attacks, with Greek resistance groups, and which involved a series of sabotage attacks on Greek rail and road networks. All of this was done to keep the German forces under pressure, and so that these diversionary actions would not make it clear where the attack on Europe would actually be launched. The date for Barkley's implementation was set for the end of July 1943, two weeks after the landings in Sicily. It was in this deception operation, which never came to fruition, that the 'Mincemeat' was included. But it too, as we shall see, without achieving the success that the 'Barkley' plan envisaged, i.e. not allowing the Germans to reinforce Sicily, which was the obvious choice of the landing.

---

2 Dwight D. Eisenhower, *Crusade in Europe*, Arnoldo Mondadori, Milan, 1949, p. 211.

It must be said that on the part of the Italian Armed Forces' General Staff and the German Commands in Italy, in particular Field Marshal Albert Kesselring Superior Commander of the South (Oberbefehlshaber Süd - OBS) who had his Headquarters in Taormina, and then in May 1943 moved to his headquarters in Frascati, at Villa Falconieri, the Allied landing operation in Sicily was expected.

And contrary to what is too often asserted and claimed with too much emphasis, especially in the United Kingdom, it did not generate any surprises in the Axis commands in Italy, since the various expedients carried out by the Allies did not help to deceive them. Not even the most famous and imaginative one, devised by Rear Admiral John Henry Godfrey, the Director of the British Naval Intelligence Service, but who had been replaced by Vice Admiral Edmund Gerard Noel Rushbrooke by the end of 1942.

On 29 September 1939, almost a month after the start of the Second World War, Rear Admiral Godfrey, released a memo of his called 'Trout', which he had studied together with one of his assistants, Lieutenant Ian Fleming, after the war famous for his novels, in particular based on the character of Agent 007, James Bond. The document contained a series of methods to be employed against the Axis powers, such as trying to lure German submarines and surface ships into minefields.

Number 28 of the 'Trout' memo list was entitled: '*A (not very nice) suggestion*'; a system that consisted in having the enemy find false documents on the corpse of an alleged courier, and which was designed for the Allied invasion plan of Sicily in 1943, in order to draw the enemy's attention to a false target from the real one. It was known to British Intelligence, particularly of their cryptographic organisation Ultra, that the Italians and Germans had foreseen three possible areas where it would be convenient for the Anglo-Americans to land: Sardinia, Sicily and Greece, after the now imminent conquest of Tunisia, as the targets of a forthcoming

▲ Field Marshal Albert Kesselring was undoubtedly considered the best commander of the German Air Force. Commander of the 2nd Air Force (Luftflotte 2), he had been sent to Italy in November 1941 by Adolf Hitler, with the post of Senior Commander of the South (OBS), and thus of all German forces in the Mediterranean, including Field Marshal Erwin Rommel's Afrika Korps. Kesselring came from the Corps of Engineers and is considered the best strategist in the Battle of Italy. In Berlin, as in Rome, he was also considered an Italophile. Despite every Anglo-American deception manoeuvre to deceive Italians and Germans from the real objective of landing in Sicily, together with Benito Mussolini and General Vittorio Ambrosio, Chief of General Staff (Comando Supremo), and General Mario Roatta, Chief of Army Staff, Kesselring was convinced, and he was right, that the invasion would take place on that large island, not falling for the constant information pitfalls devised by the Anglo-Americans.

Allied advance into southern Europe. See the map below.

Two officers were instrumental in the realisation of the plan: Charles Cholmondley, an RAF flight lieutenant seconded to MI5, the British Counterintelligence and National Security Service; and Lieutenant Commander Ewen Montagu, of the Naval Intelligence Division, where he headed NID 17 (M), the secondary branch that dealt with counterintelligence work. He was a peacetime lawyer.

Their task, assisted by a Military Intelligence (MI6) representative of the Secret Intelligence Service (SIS), the UK's foreign intelligence agency, Major Frank Foley, was to find the body of a man who had died in England of pneumonia.

They found him in London's St Pancras Hospital in Glyndwr Michael, a young Welshman of thirty-four, born in Aberbargoed on 4 January 1909 to illiterate parents, and having mental problems he had been rejected from military service, and was living in miserable conditions on a modest pension. He had died on 28 January from pulmonary oedema, probably caused by eating food with rat poison containing phosphorus, which had caused his lungs to become so saturated with water that he was unable to breathe. With the consent of his family, he was dressed in military uniform under the name of a fictitious *Major William Hynd Norrie Martin of the Royal Marines*.

The hope was that once Martin's body had been found by the Spaniards, and the autopsy examiner having ascertained that the corpse had water in the lungs, the ruse was to make people believe that, whoever had found him, that British officer had died of drowning, and that the documents he carried in a briefcase, including two letters from senior officers mentioning two landing sites, were true.

His death was faked as 'caused by drowning', which occurred while he was flying a plane that had crashed into the sea near the Atlantic coast of southern Spain with false confidential documents. Montagu and Cholmondley learned from a pathologist, Bernard Spilsbury, that the death of those who died in a plane crash was often caused by shock and not drowning, and the lungs would not necessarily fill with water. In the autopsy of a man who had died of drowning, it was unlikely that the difference between the fluid in the lungs, which had begun to decompose, and seawater would be noticed.

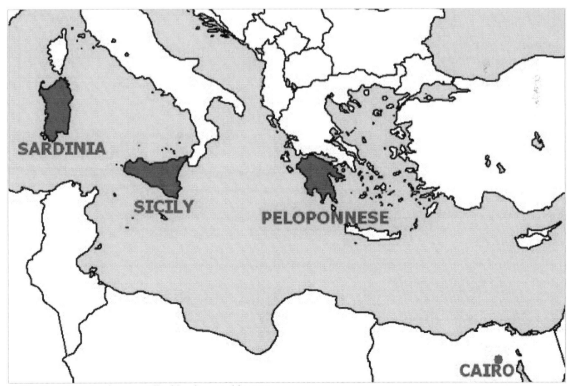

▲ The three targets where an Allied landing could occur.

However, *Spilsbury* added that '*the Spanish, as Roman Catholics, were opposed to autopsy and did not practice it unless the cause of death was of great importance*'. The choice of the Spanish coast was due to the fact that under the Franco government there were good relations with the Germans, and it was hoped that the Germans through their agents would immediately learn of the discovery of the body of a British officer, and move to learn from the Spaniards why.

In preparing the deception, Lieutenant Commander Montagu outlined three criteria for the main letter containing details of the forged plans to land in the Balkans, and the chosen location was Morea, Greece, under Italian control, where there were two important airfields. The target, named Operation Husky (the code name for the actual landing in Sicily), was to be identified casually but clearly, and was to name Sicily and another location, the Dodecanese, as the disguised landings. The correspondence had to be unofficial, as it was normally sent by diplomatic courier or by coded document.

Lieutenant General Archibald Edward Nye, Deputy Chief of the Imperial General Staff, with a profound knowledge of the ongoing military operations, was persuaded to personally write the fake main letter in which General Harold Rupert Leofric George Alexander, Deputy Commander of the Allied Command in Algiers and Commander of the 18th Army Group (7[a] US and 8[a] British) that was to land in Sicily from North Africa, was the supposed recipient.

The letter dealt with several allegedly sensitive topics, such as the awarding of medals by the Americans to British servicemen serving with them, with some unflattering comments, and the appointment of a new commander of the Guards Brigade. The most important part of the letter (see Document No. 2) stated[3] :

"*We have recent information that the Germans have been reinforcing and strengthening their defences in Greece and Crete and the C.I.G.S.* [Imperial Chief of Staff General Alan Brooke] *felt that our landing forces were insufficient. It was agreed by the Chiefs of Staff that the 5th Division should be reinforced by a group of brigades for the landing at the beach south of CAPO ARAXOS and that a similar reinforcement should be made for the 56th Division at KALAMATA*".

The second letter, hinting at an operation called 'Brimstone' (Sulphur), invented and to be located at an unspecified point in the Mediterranean, was an introduction to the fictitious Major Martin by his supposed commander, Vice Admiral Lord Louis Mountbatten, Chief of Combined Operations (and thus of landing), and addressed to Fleet Admiral Sir Andrew Browne Cunningham, Commander-in-Chief of the Allied Navies in the Mediterranean. Major Martin was referred to in the letter as an amphibious warfare expert on loan until '*the landing was completed*'. The document included a confusing reference to sardines, which Lieutenant Commander Montagu inserted into the letter in the hope that the Germans would take it to mean a planned invasion of Sardinia.

In practice, the letter, dated 21 April 1943, stated:

Dear Fleet Admiral,

I promised V.C.I.G.S. that Major Martin would organise with you the further transmission of a letter he has with him for General Alexander.
It is very urgent and very 'hot' and since it contains some observations that could not be seen by others in the War Ministry, it could not pass as a signal.
I am sure you will see that it goes ahead safely and without delay. I think you will find in Martin the man you are looking for. He is quiet and shy at first, but he really knows his stuff. He was more precise than most about the probable series of events at Dieppe and was very involved in the experiments with the latest barges and equipment that took place in Scotland.

---

3 WIKIPEDIA, *Operation Mincemeat*.

▲ Vice Admiral John Henry Godfrey, the Director of the British Naval Intelligence Service, who was responsible for the planned 'Mincemeat' operation.

▲ Lieutenant Commander Ian Lancaster Fleming, an officer in the Naval Intelligence Service and Admiral Godfrey's personal assistant. A fairly successful journalist in the post-war period, best known for creating the character of Agent 007 (James Bond).

Give him back to me, please, as soon as the assault is over. Could you bring some sardines with you: they are 'on point' here!

Yours sincerely, Louis Mountbatten

To justify the carrying of documents in the briefcase, which ran from the wrist down a sleeve of Martin's trench coat with a leather-lined basin like the one used by bank and jewellery couriers, two drafts of the official pamphlet on combined operations compiled by Hilary Aidan St George Saunders - then serving in Mountbatten's command - were added, as well as a letter from Mountbatten to Eisenhower, asking him to write a short preface for the American edition of the pamphlet. The briefcase was designed so that water would not affect the precious documents.

Also in the briefcase were: an identification card of Martin's (Admiralty number 148228), a photograph and two love letters from a non-existent fiancée named Pamela, a receipt for a diamond engagement ring costing £53 bought in a Bond Street jewellers, a letter received from a non-existent father, which included a note from the family solicitor and a message from the co-director of Lloyds Bank, Ernest Whitley Jones, requesting payment of an overdraft of £79, some personal belongings, such as a set of keys, and two items of good quality, woollen underwear.

On 13 April 1943, the Imperial Chiefs of Staff Committee met and agreed that they believed the plan should go ahead. The Committee informed Colonel John Henry Bevan, who as head of the London Controlling Section (LCS), set up in September 1941, was responsible for planning and coordinating the deception operations. Colonel Bevan said he needed to get final approval from the Prime Minister. Two days later, he met Winston

▲ The then Lieutenant-Captain of Naval Intelligence Ewen Montegu was the main originator of Operation Mincemeat. After the war, his book on the operation was a major success.

▲ RAF Lieutenant Charles Cholmondeley, of the British Security Service MI5. Together with Montagu he is considered to be among the main architects of Operation Mincemeat.

Churchill in his War Cabinet office and explained the plan to him, warning him, however, that there were several aspects that could go wrong, including the fact that the Spanish could return the corpse to the British, with the documents unread. Churchill gave his approval to the operation, but delegated final confirmation to General Dwight David Eisenhower, the Commander-in-Chief of Allied Forces in the Mediterranean, whose plan to invade Sicily could be compromised. Colonel Bevan sent a coded telegram to Eisenhower's headquarters in Algiers, requesting final confirmation to implement the proposed plan, which was received on 17 April. Meanwhile, Glyndwr Michael's corpse had been left for three months in cold storage, before being dressed as an officer and transferred to south-west Scotland encased, with dry ice to prevent disintegration, in a large cylinder marked 'Handle with care. Optical instruments'.

Having arrived at its destination, the corpse of the man who had by then become Major Martin was embarked on the British submarine *Seraph* (Lieutenant-Lieutenant Norman Limbury Auchinleck Jewell), which on 19 April 1943 left the base at Holy Loch in south-west Scotland, officially bound for Gibraltar. The *Seraph sailed* south across the Irish Sea, escorted with anti-submarine duties by the corvette *Acanthus*, part of the British Escort Group B6, entered the Atlantic and continued sailing alone, passing off the Iberian coast until it reached a position south of Lisbon, near Huelva, 1,500 metres from the coastal town of Portil Pilar.

On the night of 29-30 April, Martin's body was dumped at sea near the coast by the *Seraph*, which had travelled 12 miles from the point of the dive. And as the planners of the 'Mincemeat' had accurately calculated the motion of the current, floating with the lifebuoy he went aground near Huelva, north of Cadiz. According to Montegu, t h e area of Huelva was chosen because agent Adolf Clauss, of the Abwehr (the Secret Service of the High Command of the German Armed Forces (Oberkommando der Wehrmacht - OKW) lived there and was considered a very capable element who had excellent contacts with some Spanish officers. He was the son of the German consul, and operated under the cover of an agricultural technician. Furthermore, the British vice-consul in the city, Francis Haselden, was considered '*a reliable and helpful man*' who could be relied upon. While the submarine, which conveyed to the British Admiralty '*Operation Mincemeat completed*', continued its navigation reaching Gibraltar on 30 April, on the morning of that same day, at around 09.30, Martin's corpse floating off the beach of La Bota (Huelva) was found by a Spanish fisherman, of Portuguese origin,

▲ Pathologist Bernard Spilsbury.

In reply, quote S.R. 1924

COMBINED OPERATIONS HEADQUARTERS,
1A, RICHMOND TERRACE,
WHITEHALL, S.W

Telephone
Whitehall 9772

21st April,
1 9 4 3.

Dear Admiral of the Fleet,

I promised V.C.I.G.S. that Major Martin would arrange with you for the onward transmission of a letter he has with him for General Alexander. It is very urgent and very "hot" and as there are some remarks in it that could not be seen by others in the War Office, it could not go by signal. I feel sure that you will see that it goes on safely and without delay.

I think you will find Martin the man you want. He is quiet and shy at first, but he really knows his stuff. He was more accurate than some of us about the probable run of events at Dieppe and he has been well in on the experiments with the latest barges and equipment which took place up in Scotland.

Let me have him back, please, as soon as the assault is over. He might bring some sardines with him - they are "on points" here!

Yours sincerely

Louis Mountbatten

Admiral of the Fleet Sir A.B. Cunningham, G.C.B.,D.S.O.,
Commander in Chief Mediterranean,
Allied Force H.Q.,
Algiers.

▲ The original of the letter to Fleet Admiral Andrew Browne Cunningham.

▲ Major Francis Edward Foley, the Military Intelligence (MI6) representative of the Secret Intelligence Service (SIS), the UK's foreign intelligence agency, who was assigned to assist the work of Ewen Montegu and Charles Cholmondeley. Foyle was a famous figure. Before the war, as a passport control officer for the British embassy in Berlin, after Kristallnacht (8-9 November 1938), which took place in Germany due to the assassination attempt in Paris by 17-year-old Polish-Jewish Herschel Grynszpan against German diplomat Ernst Eduard von Rath, and before the outbreak of the Second World War, he helped thousands of Jewish families escape from Germany under the Nazi regime. He is officially recognised as a British Holocaust Hero and Righteous Among the Nations.

▼ Major General Archibald Edward Nye, Deputy Chief of the Imperial General Staff.

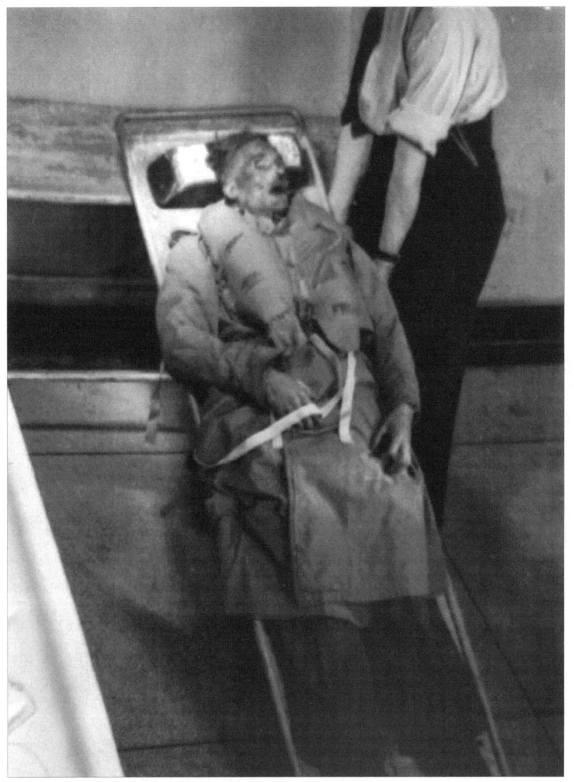

▲ The corpse of Glyndwr Michael, dressed as the false Major William Martin, strapped onto a mortuary stretcher in Hackney mortuary. Looking at Glynwr Michael's body and face, one notices his clenched hand and discoloured upper face; they are evidence of phosphorus poisoning.

▲ The same suit and briefcase worn by actor Charles Fraser-Smith in the 1956 film. He played the inventor who designed the container to transport Martin's body.

from the city of Punta Umbria, José Antonio Rey María. The fisherman recognised the British military uniform, and the corpse was brought to Huelva by Spanish soldiers, where it was handed over to the local naval examining magistrate, Mariano Pascual del Pobil, who was the first custodian of the body and the briefcase with the documents that the unidentified corpse had tied to his wrist.

On 1 May, at noon, an autopsy was performed by coroner Eduardo Fernández del Torno. British Vice Consul F.K. Hazeldene attended, and the death certificate stated *'asphyxiation by immersion in the sea'*. The corpse was then buried on 2 May, with full honours, in the 5ª San Marco section of the Spanish town's Nuestra Señora cemetery.

The documents, which were intended by the planners of Operation 'Mincemeat' to disguise the landing in Sicily, were seized by the Spanish on 5 May and sent to Madrid, where the briefcase was opened under pressure from Admiral Wilhelm Canaris, Head of the Abwehr (the German military intelligence service), whose intervention had been requested by Karl-Erich Kühlenthal, one of the Abwehr's most senior and efficient representatives in Spain. The envelopes with the letters were opened and then carefully resealed after the documents had been photographed, and the originals were returned on 11 May to Haselden with the briefcase that was sent to London. A copy was handed over to Kühlenthal (initials K O), who personally took it to Berlin, after making a telegraphic summary of the documents, which were discussed at a conference on 7 May with Admiral Dönitz, who in addition to being the Commander of the Kriegsmarine was also the Head of the Seekriegsleitung (SKL), the Directorate of Naval Operations of the German Navy, in which it was reported[4]:

▲ British writer Hilary Aidan St George Saunders.

4 *Kriegstagebuch der Seekriegsleitung/Operationsabteilung*, part A [KTB 1.Skl, A], Berlin- Bonn-Herford, Mittler & Sohn, 1988 ff., vol. 45: *Mai 1943*, 07.05.1942, pp. 127-128. The translations from German are by Augusto De Toro. My most affectionate thanks go to my friend.

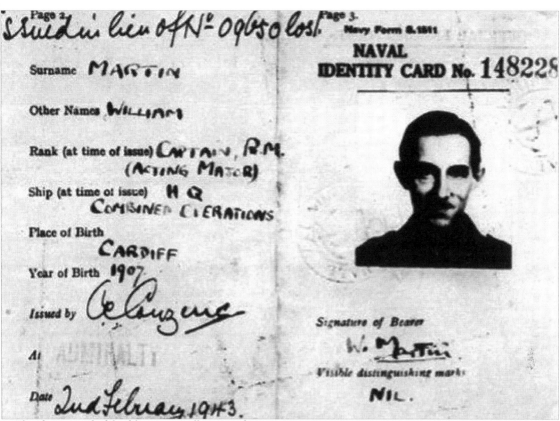

▲ The identity card of the fake Major William Hynd Norrie Martin.

▼ The photograph of Pamela, Major Martin's phantom fiancée. She was Joan Leslie, a young secretary working in the office of Lieutenant Commander Montagu.

"A British courier that crashed in Spain carried a personal letter from the Deputy Chief of Staff General to General Alexander dated 23.04 with the following content:

1) Two landing operations are planned. Codenamed Husky and Brimstone.

2) Husky seems to be about Greece. In any case, it is planned to reinforce the 5th Division for an attack [landing] at Cape Araxas and the 36th Division at Calamata.

3) Brimstone seems to be about a western Mediterranean operation,

4) For Operation Husky, diversionary actions are proposed in the Dodecanese, for Operation Brimstone diversionary actions in Sicily.

We cannot yet pronounce on the authenticity of the document. The General Staff of the Armed Forces [Generalstab des Heeres] is verifying to what extent the above-mentioned departments may correspond to the expressed intentions".

On the morning of 10 May, as we shall see, the information was forwarded by the 1st Division of the Seekriegsleitung (1/SKL) to the German Naval Command in Italy, and from there immediately brought to the attention of Supermarina, the operational organ of the Regia Marina General Staff.

From the SKL Diary, we know that on 11 May, at another conference with the Chief of the Seekriegsleitung, with an exposition by the Chief of the 3rd Information Analysis Department (3/SKL), Captain Norbert von Baumbach, it was brought to his attention that *the letters received on the courier that had crashed in Spain* were to be *"considered authentic and that the landing intentions reported therein are possible with regard to the sites and forces indicated*[5]*"*.

On the afternoon of the same day, the Grand Admiral Dönitz, who was about to leave for Rome for an important meeting with Supermarina, conferred with the Führer *'about his next intentions in the Mediterranean'*. During the discussion with Admiral Dönitz, Hitler said that he intended to maintain possession of Sardinia *'by all means'*. At the time, the German forces there were small. Instead, he considered *'an invasion of Sicily less likely*[6] *'*.

The following day, 12 May, another conference at the Chief of the Seekriegsleitung specified[7] :

"The courier documentation captured in Spain is undoubtedly authentic. The letters are currently being carefully examined and suggest that only part of the operations or diversionary operations are being dealt with".

At a new conference on 13 May, it was brought to light what documents and objectives the British intended to implement[8] :

"The Chief of 3/Skl reports as follows on the documents captured in Spain. They are:

1) A letter from the war office in London to General Alexander dated 23 April dealing with the 'Husky' and 'Brimstone' landing operations.

2) A letter from Lord Mountbatten to Admiral Cunningham,

3) A letter from Lord Mountbatten to General Eisenhower.

It follows from the first letter that a larger operation is to take place in the western Mediterranean, in conjunction with which Sicily is to be attacked as a diversion, and a landing is mentioned at two points in the Peloponnese with a diversionary action on the Dodecanese.

It appears from the second letter that the main landing in the western Mediterranean will apparently take place in Sardinia.

In the opinion of the General Staff of the Army the documents are undoubtedly authentic; however, they apparently deal only with collateral operations in relation to the main landing, which was presumably to be expected in Sardinia. ...

---

5 *Ibid.*
6 KTB 1.Skl, A, vol. 45, 11.05.1943, p. 209 and 211.
7 KTB 1.Skl, A, vol. 45, 12.05.1943, p. 225-226.
8 KTB 1.Skl, A, vol. 45, 13.05.1943, pp. 240-241.

▲ The real planners of Operation 'Mincemeat': the members of Section 17M, of the British Naval Intelligence Service's counter-intelligence. Ewen Montegu is the second sitting from the right.

▼ The London Controlling Section.

▲ The Commander of the London Controlling Section, Colonel John H. Bevan.

The Commander of the German Navy in Italy, the Southern Group and Admiral Aegean were briefly informed of the contents of the documents.
The code names mean: 'Husky' landing in the Peloponnese, 'Brimstone' landing in the western Mediterranean'.

***

In Berlin, the Foreign Office/Counter-Intelligence Office of the Supreme High Command (Oberkommando der Wehrmacht - OKW), the Army High Command's Foreign Armies West Department (Oberkommando des Heeres - OKH) and the Information Analysis Department of the Naval High Command (Seekriegsleitung - SKL), according to their own calculations of the availability of enemy naval forces, doubted that the Allies could carry out the two recalled landings in the Peloponnese and Sardinia. Even Hitler and the OKW were now firmly convinced that the enemy would attack Sardinia in the western Mediterranean and the Peloponnese in the eastern Mediterranean. General Hiroshi Oshima, the Japanese ambassador in Berlin, considered an enemy landing in Sardinia more likely than in Sicily.

In Rome, Mussolini, Kesselring and Admiral Friedrich Oskar Ruge, Commander of the German Navy in Italy, who even before Admiral Dönitz's arrival on 13 May were still unaware of the discovery of the British documents, expressed, on the contrary, the opinion that Sicily was more directly threatened than Sardinia, without, however, supporting this assumption with any sure evidence or well-founded arguments.

▲ 8 June 1943, Conference at Allied Headquarters in Algiers. British Prime Minister Winston Churchil discusses the presentation of the landing plan for the invasion of Sicily. The main military leaders are present. From left, British Foreign Secretary Anthony Eden, General Alan Brooke, Chief of the Imperial General Staff, Air Marshal Arthur Tedder Commander of the RAF, Admiral A.B. Cunningham Commander of the Allied Naval Forces, General Harold Alexander, Commander of the 18th Anglo-American Army Group, General George Marshall, Chief of the US Armed Forces, General Dwight Eisenhower, Commander-in-Chief of the Allied Forces, and General Bernard Montgomery, Commander of the British 8th Army.

▲ Charles Cholmondely, in RAF uniform, and Ewen Montagu, in Royal Navy uniform, transport Major Martin's body by truck to Scotland on 17 April 1943.

▼ The Commander, Lieutenant Commander Norman Limbury Auchinlech Jewell, and his four officers of the British submarine Seraph, selected for Operation 'Mincemeat'. The picture is from December 1943.

▲ The turret of the British submarine *Seraph* selected for Operation 'Mincemeat'. Second from right Lieutenant Commander Norman Limbury Auchinleck Jewell.

▼ The British corvette *Acanthus*, which escorted the submarine *Seraph* in the Irish Sea.

▲ Huelva, north of Cadiz, where the corpse of the fake Major Martin was found on the beach.

▼ The corpse of the phantom Major Martin is examined by the Spaniards. From a scene in the film *"The Man Who Never Was"*.

In the SKL Diary, a precise report submitted by the Foreign Office/Counterintelligence Office of the OKW on 19 May explained how the British documents had ended up in Spanish hands and how they had been handled with special systems, so that after viewing, it was not recognised how the envelopes with the papers had been opened. The documents had then been returned to the British in their original state through the Spanish Foreign Ministry[9].

But these precautions were not enough, and the British, who had placed eyelashes inside the envelopes that were missing, soon realised, to their great satisfaction, that the envelopes had been opened and that the contents were known to the Spaniards, and they guessed that the information would reach the Germans, as was later confirmed by the cryptographic source Ultra.

Thus, this essential part of the 'Mincemeat' operation had flatly succeeded. Later, in a conference at the SKL Chief, it was brought to light that the documents were in the bag of a deceased officer, Major Martin. The British consul was present when they were found, but the Spaniards had seized them and returned them.

Still on 30 May, again according to the SKL Diary, there was the belief in that body '*that the next major operations of the enemy are to be expected around mid-June against Sardinia and Corsica in the western Mediterranean and, in the eastern Mediterranean, against the Peloponnese with its centre of gravity in the eastern Mediterranean*[10]'.

▲ Personal items found by the Spanish on the body of Major Martin.

---

9 Prot. 1.Skl. 14712/43, in KTB, part C, binder XIV.
10 KTB 1.Skl, A, vol. 45, 30.05.1943, p. 514.

▲ Admiral Wilhelm Canaris, Chief of the Abwehr.

CHAPTER 2

GERMAN CONCERNS IN BERLIN AND THE IMPORTANT CONSIDERATIONS OF ANGLO-AMERICAN HISTORIANS

On Operation 'Mincemeat', the great US historian, Professor Admiral Samuel Eliot Morison was very precise in the details of the British plan, and also very pungent, writing down the essentials. When the Commander-in-Chief of the German Navy, Grand Admiral Karl Dönitz, returned from Rome on 13 May 1943 [actually on the 14th], where there had been a conference with the heads of the Italian Royal Navy, he presented himself to Hitler [at 5.30 p.m.] to also report on a conversation he had had with Benito Mussolini, "*he found the Führer transformed by the discovery of an Anglo-American plan*". It reported, as he had been told, that '*Allied attacks would be directed mainly against Sardinia and the Peloponnese*', according to a very elaborate British naval plan called 'Mincemeat'[11].

According to Morison[12] :

"*The key documents were:*
1)   A 'letter' from the Deputy Chief of the General Staff to General Alexander, informing him that Sicily was a mere protest, a diversion from Operation Husky. The real target was the Dodecanese [sic];
2)   A 'letter' from Admiral Moutbatten to Admiral Cunningham, presenting Major Martin as an expert on landings and adding: 'Send him back to me, please, as soon as the assault is over: he might bring some sardines with him![13] '
The experts in the Teutonic intelligence service deduced from this laborious play on words, as they thought they would, that Sardinia was also a target in the Husky. Hitler himself was completely misled.
As a result, in June extensive supplies of good troops and equipment were shipped from the Adriatic and French ports to the Peloponnese, an armoured division [it was the 90th Panzer Grenadier Division] was sent to Sardinia, coastal batteries were installed on the Greek coast, and German minelayers, which were already laying mines off the southern coast of Sicily, were diverted for Greece, along with most of the torpedo boats then in Sicilian waters [sic]. On 21 May, the German Army High Command informed Marshal Kesselring that 'the measures to be taken in Sardinia and the Peloponnese must take precedence over any other....
However, in contrast to the credulity of Hitler and the men around him, the responsible Italian admirals and German generals acted **with common sense and decisiveness** *[boldface is by Aurore] The Italian Intelligence Service first discredited 'Major Martin', and Supermarina's 'view' of 24 June ruled out Greece; the deployment of Allied landing forces, it said, proved that the safe target was Sicily. Marshal Kesselring did not take the imaginary Major into account either. On 20 June he began to send the Herman Göring armoured division to Sicily through the Straits of Messina, in reinforcement of the Sicilian garrison [15ª Panzergrenadier Division and other units]; and his 'point of view' on 28 June foresees the landing in Sicily, estimates it possible in Sardinia as well, makes no mention of Greece*".

For Morison dismantles the importance of Operation 'Mincemeat', so dear to the British, and for his many distinctions on their strategy, particularly Churchill's, and it is to be understood that the British have little regard for the great American historian. His masterpiece, disliked by the Spanish, the beautiful book '*Christopher Columbus*'.

---

11 Samuel Eliot Morison, *History of United States Naval Operations in World War II, Sicily - Salerno - Anzio, January 1943 - June 1944*, Castle Books, 2001, pp. 45-47.
12 *Ibid.*
13 The Deputy Chief of the Imperial General Staff was General Archibald Edward Nye; General Harold Alexander the Deputy Chief of the Allied Command in Algiers and Commander of the 18th Army Group which was to land in Sicily; Admiral Louis Moutbatten, (cousin of England's King George VI then Viceroy of India which led to independence in 1947) the Commander of the Combined Special Operations (and thus landing); Admiral Andrew Browne Cunningham the Commander of the Allied Marines.

▲ The funeral of the non-existent Major Martin with military honours in the Huelva cemetery.

▼ Abwehr agent Karl-Erich Kühlenthal (right), the most experienced and efficient Canaris employee in Spain.

Of the same opinion as Morison is the equally great British naval historian, Captain Stephen Wentworth Roskill who, in Volume 3 of his monumental work *The War at Sea*, reports what may be considered to have set the closing slab to the tomb of Operation Mincemeat, writing[14] :

"Finally, among the measures to deceive the enemy, mention must be made of the macabre trick of putting at sea off the Spanish coast, a disguised corpse carrying forged letters from high-ranking officers and compiled in such a way as to give the impression that the attack, when it came, would be against Greece and Sardinia. Although Hitler and his close advisers were certainly deceived, **the German and Italian commanders appear to have been less naïve** [bold is Aurore's] *and* **additional reinforcements were indeed transported to Sicily towards the** *end of June*[15] '.

The same point, although more nuanced, was made by British General C.J.C. Molony, writing about Operation Mincemeat[16] :

"The plan caused a flurry of appreciation and deceived or confused many, including Hitler. The strike drew the enemy's attention to the 'wrong' end of the Mediterranean, a distraction that helped keep the real Allied plan secret. But Molony added that the 'Mincemeat': **had no effect on the Axis ground forces in Sicily on D-Day** (bold is the author's), i.e. at the time of the landings".

In fact, I must refute Playfayr, there was no lack of '*attention*' and '*distraction*' on the part of the Italian and German Commands at the eastern end of the Mediterranean, and Hitler's and the OKW's concerns, as we shall see, were justified because of the fact that there were large mineral deposits of copper, bauxite, chromium and fuel oil in Romania, which were essential to Germany's war effort. An Allied attack on the Dodecanese or Greece would have endangered all those resources, which needed to be defended. As for the threat in the western Mediterranean, the Führer believed that Sardinia could be the most threatened by the enemy, while Mussolini was firm in his opinion that the landing would take place in Sicily[17] . With this he was agreeing with the opinion of Winston Churchill who, when presented with the plan of Operation 'Mincemeat', seems to have said about the true objective of the landing: '*Everyone but a damned fool* [he was referring to Hitler] *would know that it is Sicily*[18] '.

And indeed, with the arrival in Sicily on 22-23-24 and 25 May of the Herman Göring Division, the plan of Operation 'Mincemeat' to prevent the Germans from reinforcing their forces in Sicily failed miserably. That plan, as feared by Churchill, was like a sieve, leaking water from all sides.

Finally, one cannot miss in this exposition of opinions what was written by the famous British historian B.H. Liddell Hart[19] :

---

14 Stephen Roskill, 'History of the Second World War United Kingdom Military Series', *The Mediterranean and Middle East, The Campaign in Sicily and The Campaign in Italy 3rd September 1943 to 31st March 1944*, Volume III, Part I, HMSO, London. For Roskill's note: see Ewen Montagu, *The Man Who Never Was* (Evans Bros, 1953).

15 On the evening of 13 June, the OBS, in its Operational Situation, message no. 1842/25, informed the Italians that the following day, the Hermann Göring Division would be transferred to the Potenza - Matera - Altamura area. The Division reached Sicily on 22 and 23 June, comprising: "*1a Armoured Regiment Company, Assault Company Headquarters, 8a and 9a Company 2nd Armoured Grenadier Regiment, 1st Group Anti-Aircraft Artillery Regiment, aliquots Communications Department, Repair Company, Baker Company, Administrative Office, 2a Sanitary Company, 2nd and 3rd Motorcycle Platoon, except inefficient aliquots of the Anti-Aircraft Regiment, Artillery Regiment and Supply Regiment. On day 24, all motorised and tracked vehicles will be on Sicilian territory, while presumably on day 25, the last aliquot of the Armoured Regiment will arrive in the Reggio area by express transport. A total of 42 trains. 29a Armoured Grenadier Division, and a total of 5 trains Assault Brigade "Reichsführer SS"* arrived in their own displacement areas. Considering that there was now an Anglo-American maritime situation in the Mediterranean that included 6 battleships and perhaps 3 aircraft carriers [2 safe], the document stated '*let us assume imminent decisive enemy attack operations*'. See, ASMAUS, *DCHG* Fund 3, folder 36.

16 C.J.C. Molony & F.C. Flynt - H.L. Davies - T.P. Gleave, *The Mediterranean and Middle East*, Volume V, HMSO, London, 1978, p. 37.

17 Archives of the Army General Staff Historical Office (henceforth ASMEUS), fonds *H.5*, folder 3RR.

18 Crowdy, Terry, *Deceiving Hitler: Double-Cross and Deception in World War II.*, Oxford, 2008, p. 195.

19 B.H. Liddell Hart, *Military History of World War II*, Mondadori, Milan, 1970, p. 615.

"*The corpse and the letter* [from General Nye] *were part of an ingenious plan devised by a section of the British secret service to throw the Germans off the trail. The stratagem was implemented so well that the leaders of the German secret service did not even doubt the authenticity of the documents. Although it did not change the conviction of the Italian leaders and Kesselring that Sicily would be the next Allied target*".

It is incredible how the author of the book '*The Man Who Never Was*', and the makers of the film, paid no attention to, or gave any credence to, what was written by leading Anglo-American historians, and knew nothing of the Italian and German thinking in Italy, whose greatest concern about an imminent enemy threat on European soil, after the loss of Tunisia, was directed towards Sicily; because from Sicily the invasion of the Italian peninsula could begin, and bring about the political upheavals that would lead first to the fall of Mussolini and then to the surrender of Italy.

They are still conceited enough to have produced another film in 2022, about the '*Man Who Never Was*', titled, as mentioned, '*Operation Mincemeat*[20]'.

▲ The Commanders of the Allied Forces in the Mediterranean at Algiers Headquarters, who after the end of the Tunisian campaign prepared plans for the invasion of Sicily. From left, Commander-in-Chief General Dwight David Eisenhower, Air Marshal Arthur Tedder Commander Allied Air Forces, General Harold Alexander Deputy Commander Allied Forces and Commander 15th Army Group, Admiral Andrew Browne Cunningham, Commander Allied Marines. Behind Minister Harold Macmillan, General Walter Bedell Smith, Chief of Staff of Allied Command, and an unidentified officer.

---

20 The author of this book, in his early twenties, had the opportunity to find himself doing his historical research, in the 1950s, when the Archives of the Historical Office of the Navy, was frequented by Professor Morison, both with the authorisation of the then Director, Admiral Giuseppe Fioravanzo. Morison was doing his research, which lasted a few days, in that Italian archive exactly as any researcher who has to do objective and important work must do, without fear of contradiction, otherwise he risks writing books of a shoddy nature, not entirely truthful and even fictional, with little sense of truth. Never trust publications albeit memoirs, let alone films with pathetic love scenes.

▲ Imperial Deputy Chief of Staff General Archibald Edward Nye, visiting the British 8th Army in Italy in the autumn of 1944, talks in Forlì with Australian General Bernard Freyberg, Commander of the Australian 2nd Division.

▲ Rear Admiral Louis Mountbatten, Commander-in-Chief of Combined Operations.

CHAPTER 3

THE OPINION OF THE ITALIAN AND GERMAN MILITARY LEADERSHIP IN ITALY

On 8 March 1943, with message No. 11339, the Italian Supreme Command transmitted the following message to the Army, Navy and Air Force Staffs:

"As a rule, the following information is conveyed, which O.K.W. obtained from a source that is claimed to be reliable:

1) Information gathered by the Spanish Foreign Ministry representative in Tangier, Ambassador Castilo, states that among the circulating rumours of imminent Allied operations, the one concerning a forthcoming landing action in Sardinia should be taken seriously.

2) According to this information, the Anglo-Americans intended to occupy Sardinia and use it as a base for air strikes, which in turn would have to proceed to another major operation.

Such an operation against Sardinia could be launched depending on how the situation develops, either before or after the planned operations in Tunisia. Contrary to the widely held opinion, particularly in political circles, that the creation of a second front should take place in the Balkans or Norway, or both of these countries at the same

▲ Hitler, who was concerned about defending Romania, with its large bauxite and chromium deposits and its large oil fields, vital to Germany's war economy, had been obsessed since the autumn of 1942 that the Allies might land in Greece and set up airfields there to hit Romanian targets. Thus, he was initially worried when he learned that the British intended to land in the Morea. But it does not appear that his worries increased in the following days. So much so that in the second half of May he offered Mussolini to send five new German divisions to help protect Italy and the islands of Sardinia and Corsica. If he was so afraid of Greece, he could have sent the five divisions to protect the Hellenic peninsula, but instead, he evidently considered them more useful in Italy, and to Greece, he sent only one armoured division, which arrived in Thessaloniki in June 1943. The Chief of the Italian High Command, General Ambrosio, underestimating the importance of this offer, convinced Mussolini to tell Hitler that only three divisions were accepted, to be deployed one in Sicily, one in Sardinia and one on the Italian peninsula. Later, in mid-June 1943, when Sicily and the Italian peninsula appeared as the next Allied objective, the Supreme Command requested the OKW to transfer the two German divisions to southern Italy. The 16th and 26th Armoured Divisions arrived.

▲ Two great naval historians objectively described what the final outcome of Operation Mincemeat was. On the left Professor Admiral Samuel Eliot Morison, on the right Captain Stephen Wentworth Roskill.

▼ Panzer IV G tanks of the 1st Armoured Division (General Walter Krüger) transferred in June 1943 from Rennes (France) to Greece. In the picture the Division is in Thessaloniki with 60 type IV G tanks. In June it received the Wespe and Hummel self-propelled tanks, becoming fully operational at the end of the month.

time, a member of the Secret Service currently in Lisbon opines that it would always be the intention to strike the main blow against Italy".

While erroneous and false news about the intentions of the Allies followed one another, generating alarms, but also suspicions of deception, and in Berlin there was uncertainty as to where the enemy would land, since they believed that areas in Europe ranging from Norway to the Aegean Sea were under threat, Supermarina had not failed to notice that the enemy's attention, through aerial bombardment, was directed towards Sicily, with the western and southern parts of the island being probable landing areas. as shown by what is written in one of his memos of 4 April 1943, which I quote below in its full form[21]:

SUPERMARINA
6 April 1943-XXI

POSSIBLE TARGETS FOR AN ENEMY LANDING IN SICILY

1) In relation to the enemy air offensive over Sicily, it is noted that bombing raids were carried out in force, with a decidedly destructive purpose, only on the ports of Messina and Palermo. On the other hand, the current great importance of the port of Trapani as a departure base for Tunisia and a support point for convoys in transit cannot have escaped the enemy, nor the heavy concentration of ships that often occurs in that port. Similarly, the activity of the smaller vessels in the port of Marsala and Porto Empedocle could not have escaped the enemy. It therefore seems to be worth considering the fact that no sensible bombardment was carried out against these ports, as well as the other minor ports in southern Sicily.
2) Therefore, unless these bombardments are carried out in the near future, it is believed that the lack of enemy offence on these ports should be attributed to the need that the enemy may have of them in the future, and therefore be considered not only as a confirmation of the enemy's planned place of attack on Sicily, but even as an indication of the areas in which the landings would take place and should then be fuelled, namely the Trapani-Marsala areas and the southern coast of the island.

In a memo on the talks in Klessheim (Salzburg), between representatives of the Italian Supreme Command and the OKW, it is stated, among other things[22] :

"Regarding the Mediterranean problems, German concern is limited to that which can be had for a theatre of war of secondary importance. One sees the necessity of holding Tunisia at any cost, in order to bind the forces of the enemy as long as possible; a landing in Sardinia and Sicily is feared, and one is disposed to assure all possible concurrence, but there is a tendency not to devote available means to chess-boards which are not at present active in the expectation that they will be attacked. A landing on the southern coast of France is not considered probable; a landing in Greece is also seen as not imminent, and in relation to the attitude of Turkey. It is believed that the latter will wait a long time before moving, as Bulgaria - by King Boris' recent declaration - would go to war against it. Turkey is also a manoeuvring element in British hands, against any excessive and dangerous Russian claims".

On 3 May 1943, with the document protocol No. 127711/OP with the subject '*General Situation - Orientations*', sent to the highest commanders of the Italian Armed Forces at a time when plans for the defence of Sardinia and Sicily were being implemented under the direction of the Supreme Command, General Vittorio Ambrosio, Chief of the General Staff, had written[23] :

"We must consider it possible that the enemy intends to attempt a landing in force in the western Mediterranean even before occupying Tunisia: the French Mediterranean coast and Sardinia are particularly exposed, the eventual loss of which would mean the fall of Corsica and would give the enemy the necessary bases to act against the peninsula. Having mastered Tunisia, the enemy could instead attempt the occupation of Sicily and thus open up

---

21 Archivio Ufficio Storico Marina Militare (from now on AUSMM), Fondo *Promemoria di Supermarina*, folder 2.
22 ASMEUS, *General Conduct of the War (Impressions from the various interviews - 7-10 April 1943-XXI)*.
23 Historical Diary of the Supreme Command, Documents, May 1943.

transit in the Mediterranean, to then turn towards the Aegean and Balkania'. In this situation, the preparation of the defence of the Italian coasts (Sardinia, Corsica, Sicily, the Peninsula) and, in collaboration with the Allied forces, that of the French Mediterranean coast, becomes of paramount importance for us ... The external threat of an attempt to land in Balkania appears less imminent ...".

On 6 May 1943, during a meeting at Palazzo Venezia at the Duce's, attended by General Ambrosio, Marshal Kesselring, his Chief of Staff, General Siegfried Westphal, and General Paul Deichmann, Chief of Staff of the 2ª Luftflotte, the problems concerning the defence of Italian territory were discussed. Kesselring reported that he had asked the Führer 'to send troops to reinforce the defence in the Mediterranean', and Hitler replied that he was sending a division and had given the order to reconstitute the Herman Göring Division, with the divisions that were to go to Tunisia and remained in Italy. Three divisions would then be available. Asked by Mussolini 'What kind of divisions are these?', Westphal replied: 'One for Sicily motorised, one in Italy equipped to carry a single regiment, stationed in Taranto, Naples, Livorno, one in Sardinia partly motorised'. Field Marshal Kesselring added: 'But in Sicily there are also 56 tanks of which 16 Tiger', to which was added, at Mussolini's request and Westphal's reply, '25 tanks ready to be transported to Sardinia'.

For his part, Field Marshal Kesselring had realised that Sicily represented the only obstacle that would prevent the Allies from landing on the Italian peninsula through the Strait of Messina, while Sardinia, about which there were still Italian and Berlin uncertainties, could not give great advantages from an operational point of view since its eventual conquest would not have brought the Anglo-Americans closer to the boot. The possibility of a simultaneous landing in Sicily and Sardinia was also ruled out, because this would have involved the use of forces that the Allies did not have at that time. Linking the news of the aerial reconnaissance with those communicated by the agents stationed in enemy territories, which among other things indicated the presence in Malta of three battalions of paratroopers, Kesselring was convinced that the next Anglo-American objective would be Sicily. Contributing to this conviction was the Axis aerial reconnaissance of the anchorages in French North Africa, which in June 1943 ascertained the presence of 548 landing units (capable of transporting 44,600 men and 3,610 vehicles), 45 per cent of which were located in the Oran-Algeri area, 34 per cent in the Bougie Bona area and 21 per cent in the Bizerte-Tunis area. To all this was added the presence at Malta's airports of some 400 aircraft, evidently to be used to support the landing operations, to which were added hundreds more in nearby Tunisia and the conquered island of Pantelleria, on whose beaches the British landed on 10 June[24].

***

Let us now see how the Italians learnt what the real aims of Operation Mincemeat were, based on two documents, dated 8 May, which, until I wrote my essay 'The Man Who Never Was' for the *academia.edu* website in 2021, had remained unpublished[25].

Of the discovery of the documents brought by Major Martin, Supermarina was immediately informed by the German Traffic Protection Office of the German Navy Command in Italy, with the hand-delivered message 1905 of 04.00 hours on 10 May 1943. The German Navy's premises were located next to Supermarina's, and had been moved from the Palazzo Marina on the Lungotevere delle Navi in Santa Rosa (Rome - La Storta), on the Via Cassia, where Supermarina's campaign headquarters, now the Naval Squadron Headquarters, was located.

The disputed message was transmitted from the 1st Division of the Seekriegsleitung in Berlin at 9.55 p.m. on 9 May, and read as follows:

24 Francesco Mattesini, *La partecipazione tedesca alla Guerra aeronavale nelMediterraneo (1940-1945)"* (co-author for the political part Alberto Santoni), Edizioni dell'Ateneo & Bizzarri, Rome, 1980 (2ª Edition, Alberelli, Parma, 2005), p. 292-293.

* Wrote the British historian G.A. Shepperd in his fine book *The Italian Campaign 1943-14945*, p. 43, that: "*Kesselring was convinced that the Allies would limit their attacks to the effective range of ground-based fighters, and that they would strike Sicily rather than Sardinia, as a possible prelude to an advance across the Italian peninsula towards the Balkans. German troops were therefore disposed accordingly'.*

25 Francesco Mattesini, *The Man Who Never Existed*. In reference to the film *L'uomo che non è mai esistito*. The 'Mincemeat' operation that did not fool the Axis Commands in Italy, Rome, November 2021, on the Author's page of the *academia edu* website.

Reserved for the person:

K O in Spain reports that an English courier has been grounded in Spain. He was carrying a personal letter from the Chief of the Imperial General Staff addressed to General Alexander dated 23 April.
1)   Two landing companies are planned, named HUSKY et BRIMSTONE.
2)   HUSKY probably means Greece. In any case, the 5th Division was expected to be reinforced to attack Cape ARAXAS and the 56th Division to attack Calamata.
3)   BRIMSTONE probably means an enterprise in the western Mediterranean.
4)   A dummy enterprise on the Dodecanese and a dummy enterprise on Sicily are planned for the company HUSKY.

K O in Spain will send copies of the originals.

The following is the original of the letter about the 'Mincemeat' operation that the Germans, via the 1/SKL, had promptly transmitted to Rome at 9.55 p.m. on 9 May 1943:

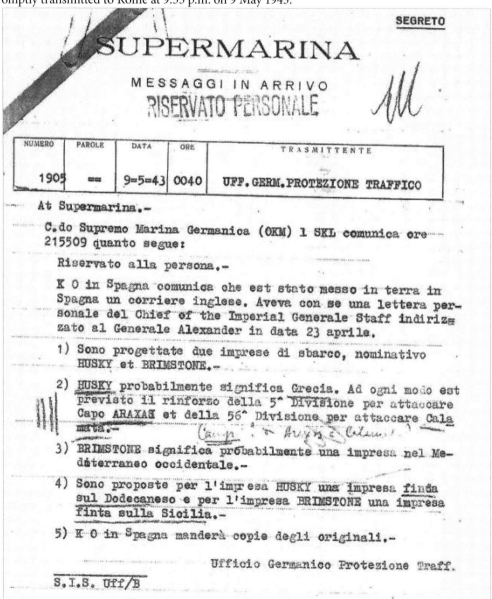

On this subject, a British historical writer, Ben Macintyre, wrote: '*A British spy in Italian government circles had reported that information about the mincemeat had reached Rome "through the Spaniards and not directly through the Germans". He confirmed that the Spanish General Staff had made their own copies of the documents and passed them on to the Italians.* '*The Italian High Command has the details of the letter and has accepted it as genuine'. The Italian ambassador in Madrid told the Germans that he had obtained the 'information from an absolute irrefutable source that the enemy intends to carry out landing operations in Greece in the very near future'. The German ambassador had passed on the news, now no longer new, to Berlin. This is an intriguing way of commenting on the state of the Axis alliance, namely that the Italians had handed over this high-level information to the Germans, but the Germans, who had known this for much longer, did not feel obliged to share it with their Italian allies.*

Reading all this, the reader, particularly Anglo-Saxon readers, can get an idea of how far the manipulation and lividity of those who are at least ill-informed historians can go.

The text of the document, which was, however, incomplete, since it was the content of one of the two letters, the most important one from General Edward Nye, clearly stated that the landing in Sicily would only take place as a diversion, as well as the one in the Dodecanese, since the objective was instead indicated in coastal locations in the Morea (western Greece), where there were important airfields with Italian fighter planes for the protection, in the eastern Ionian Sea, of naval traffic between Italy and Greece. It is important to emphasise that the document reported that copies of the originals of the documents had been sent to Rome (which was done), which belies any other inference.

Supermarina, under whose direction was the Navy Chief of Staff Admiral Luigi Sansonetti, also following the arrival of other information from Spain, which was also dated 9 May 1943 and was, moreover, misleading, immediately drew up a letter for the Supreme Command, which, however, was not sent, evidently due to the decision of the Undersecretary of State and Chief of Staff of the Regia Marina, Admiral Arturo Riccardi, who was supposed to have drawn it up.

Since it is also a document of the utmost importance for us to understand what Sansonetti's opinion was at the time, who remained convinced that the fake letter sent by the SKL was true, he reproduced it below in its original form[26] :

"*Operational intentions of the enemy.*

SECRET - CONFIDENTIAL - PERSONAL

1.   The three enclosed pieces of information are particularly reliable.

2.   The first (Annex 1) and the second (Annex 2) agree that landing operations in the Western Mediterranean are imminent and that they are not directed against the coasts and islands of Spain. This leaves the coast of Provence, Sardinia and Sicily as likely targets. The intensification of air actions over the Sicilian ports, the advantages of conquering the positions in Tunisia, and the possibility of gaining control of the Sicilian Channel through the possession of western Sicily would lead to the conclusion that this was the operation the enemy would attempt first. However, the current deployment of landing craft is better prepared for an attack on Sardinia[27] .As long as this deployment is not modified and as long as work is not carried out to make Tunisia's naval and air positions even partially effective (dredging - even partial opening of the ports and airports), it must be assumed that the enemy's first objective is Sardinia and that any actions against Sicily (such as the air actions of 8-9 May) are a feint or have other contingent purposes (to make it difficult for our forces concentrated on the Capo Bon peninsula to be refuelled and protected by air).

26 AUSMM, *Admiral Sansonetti's memo*, folder no. 2.

27 The Allied deployment in Morocco and Tunisia was logical since there was still fighting in Tunisia, with German and Italian forces reduced between Bizerte and the Cape Bon Peninsula. They would surrender on 12 and 13 May.

3.	This appreciation is confirmed in the third piece of information (Appendix 3), which envisages two landing operations, one in the Western Mediterranean, with a feint towards Sicily and an unspecified main target, but which it seems logical to assume is Sardinia, and one in the Eastern Mediterranean, which would include a feint against the Dodecanese and an effective action against the Morea aimed at occupying the airfields of Araxos and Calamata. These clarifications make the information particularly reliable. The operation in the eastern Mediterranean directed against the weakest area of our deployment for the conquest of targets of primary importance for subsequent air operations is highly probable. However, a prior concentration of naval transport and convoy escort units in the Levant is necessary for such an operation. The outflow of such units through the Sicilian Channel takes some time and, in any case, should not go unnoticed.

4.	In conclusion, as things stand, one must assume that an operation directed at the occupation of Sardinia is imminent, while operations towards other targets are less likely.

THE CHIEF OF STAFF"

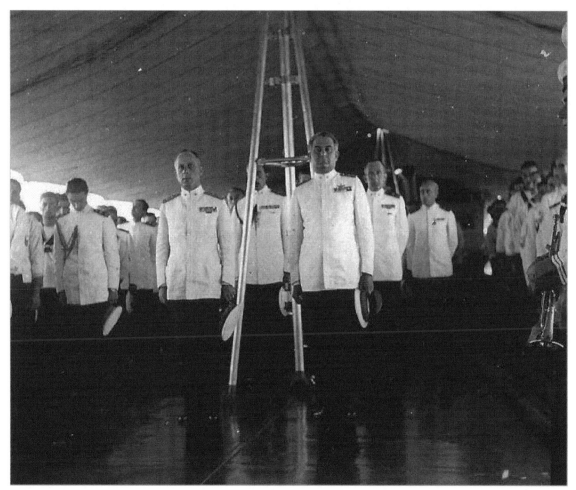

▲ In the front left, Admiral Luigi Sansonetti, Sub-Chief of Staff of the Regia Marina, pictured here commanding the 7th Naval Division. On his right, Captain Francesco Rogadeo, commander of the cruiser *Muzio Attendolo*.

The three mentioned Annexes (see Document No. 4) were dated 9 May 1943. The first one, which arrived by message No. 33877 from a German trustee source, stated:

An Anglo-American landing operation is believed to be imminent (even at the end of the week) targeting southern France aut the Tyrrhenian islands [Sardinia and Sicily].

The second attachment that arrived with message No. 33874 stated:

Particularly reliable source reports that Admiral Gibraltar in conversation with Spanish officer hinted that landing est a matter of days (halt) It is strongly believed that operations against territories aut Spanish islands should be ruled out.

The third attachment, was the one sent by the SKL, which in the unshipped letter from Supermarina was considered reliable for the landing in Sardinia and also in the Morea.

It is to be assumed that Sansonetti's opinion was not shared by Admiral Arturo Riccardi, who did not believe that Sardinia was a safe target for the expected enemy landing. Being of the same opinion as Mussolini, Kesselring, Admiral Friedrich Ruge, Commander of the German Navy in Italy, General Vittorio Ambrosio, Chief of the General Staff (Comando Supremo), and General Mario Roatta, Commander of the 6ª Army in Sicily (later replaced by General Alfredo Guzzoni and promoted on 1 June to Army Chief of Staff), Riccardi was convinced that the Allies' primary intention would be Sicily. General Ambrosio had paid a visit to Sardinia to assess the island's defences, and upon his return to Rome on 8 May, he sent a note to Mussolini informing him that the Sardinian coastline made a landing difficult, except at a couple of points, and that he did not think it likely that the Allies would land there. In addition to Sicily, the highly intelligent General Roatta considered the coasts of southern Italy to be particularly threatened, since the Allies (and he was right) could have reached the Balkans much more easily and quickly than via Crete and Rhodes[28] . Thus Ambrosio arrived at the following conclusions of a perfect analysis, well understood by Mussolini[29] :

"All things considered, I believe that there is little likelihood of an attack on Sardinia and in any case I believe that it is much less than an attempted invasion against Sicily, whose strategic position represents a much greater obstacle in the Mediterranean basin for our adversaries. The conquest of Sicily does not presuppose a further operation, but it can be an end in itself because it gives the enemy the security of movement, diminishes the commitment of his naval forces and the loss of his merchant ships: in other words, it alone represents an objective of real and pre-eminent importance to which we must strive with every effort and at every risk".

In the meantime, in Berlin, the material arrived from Madrid had been evaluated, and confidence was placed in the authenticity of the plans contained in one of the letters, naturally that of General Nye. And while the Mediterranean Commands were being warned, a meeting was held at the OKW on 11 May. As there are no documents on the meeting, we do not know what Hitler's reaction was, but on the following day the Führer, looking alarmed (according to some post-war theories), issued an order stating that the places most threatened by the enemy were, '*in the western Mediterranean Sardinia, Corsica and Sicily; in the eastern one the Peloponnese and the Dodecanese islands*', the commands entrusted with the defence of the Mediterranean were to act swiftly against any landing attempt, and that the '*measures concerning Sardinia and the Peloponnese*' were to have '*absolute precedence over everything else*[30] '.

On 12 May, the OKW warned Field Marshal Kesselring, transmitting: '*It appears from an absolutely reliable source that a large-scale enemy landing attempt will be made in the immediate future in the eastern and western Mediterranean*'. This was followed by a summary of the contents of the drowned British courier's letters, to be brought to the attention of Grand Admiral Karl Dönitz, Head of the German Navy, who was in Rome at the

---

28 Schreiber, p. 117.
29 Benito Mussolini, *Storia di un anno. Il tempo del bastone e della Carota*, Mondadori, 1944-XXIII, p. 41-42.
30 Schreiber p. 344-345.

time for a conference with Supermarina, and the Italian Supreme Command.

Also on the same day, 12 in the evening, further news arrived from the German Ambassador in Madrid, Hans-Heinrich Diekhoff, provided *'under obligation of secrecy'* by the Spanish Foreign Minister, Francisco Gómez-Jordana Sousa, about a major attack by the Americans against southern Europe within the next two weeks. It was claimed[31] :

The plan (as the informant was able to ascertain from direct sight of secret British documents) envisaged two feints against Sicily and the Dodecanese, while the real offensive would press against two main targets, Crete and the Peloponnese. Alexandria will be the enemy's most important collection point in the eastern Mediterranean, and Algiers in the western one. It appears from the document that the attack in the eastern Mediterranean will be mainly by the British and that against Italy mainly by the Americans'. ... Jordana ... specified that, taking into account the source, he believed the information to be very safe and thought it was his duty to communicate it to us.

In Rome, at the meeting held on 13 May in Palazzo Venezia at the Duce's residence, in the presence of Grand Admiral Dönitz, General Ambrosio, Admirals Giovanni Bernardi and Giuseppe Bertoldi (Naval Attaché in Berlin), and General Enno von Rintelen (Officer of the OKW at the Italian Supreme Command), Mussolini said:

"We do not know the plans of the Anglo-Americans. There is the possibility of an attack against Sicily and Sardinia. In my view Sicily is more likely ... As far as forces are concerned, we do not need men; we have them. The Führer had proposed five divisions [to be sent to Italy. I think this is too many, 3 are enough, as long as they are divisions with a lot of vehicles, which ensure rapid approaches and tanks".

To Mussolini's requests, which included sending 30 squadrons of bombing planes and 20 fighter squadrons, Hitler replied that the three divisions would be sent, that they had six tank battalions (about 300), that he would send 50 batteries (200 guns) to Sicily, and that 50 squadrons of planes would be sent to Italy (see Doc-

▲ General Vittorio Ambrosio, head of the Supreme Command, right in the photo, in agreement with Admiral Riccardi (pictured left next to Admiral Doenitz) was absolutely convinced that the Allied landing would take place in Sicily.

31 Frederick W. Deakin, *Storia della Repubblica di Salò*, (translation by Renzo De Felice), Enaudi, Turin, 1963.

▲ Admiral Arturo Riccardi, Chief of Staff of the Regia Marina, accompanies Mussolini as he reviews the crews of Italian naval units in Taranto in June 1942.

ument No. 5). After these aids, due to Field Marshal Kesselring's intervention accepted by General Ambrosio, three more divisions were sent to Italy in June, including the 1[a] paratroopers, which was in Provençal France, and two armoured divisions (16[a] and 29[a]), which were deployed in southern Italy between the Campagna and Apulia. The situation changed after 25 July with the fall of Mussolini and the arrival at the head of the government of Marshal Badoglio, At this point, Hitler, who had always been generous with his friend Mussolini as far as possible, no longer trusted the Italian leaders, and from his far-sighted point of view he was right.

On 14 May, in a conversation with Grand Admiral Dönitz, on his return from Rome[32] , Hitler said that he disagreed with Mussolini, who had been convinced that the most likely point of the enemy landing would be in Sicily, but for his part maintained his conviction that the invasion would occur mainly against Sardinia and the Peloponnese. The documents of the drowned courier confirmed this. As for the Allies' plans to invade island and southern Italy, as revealed by the many intelligence reports and representatives of friendly governments, they were nothing more than a prelude to wide-ranging landing operations along the western coasts of Greece and the Adriatic. If these operations had succeeded, they could have led to an eventual Italian collapse, which would have had serious and direct repercussions in western Europe and immediately afterwards on the southern flank of the German armies on the Russian front.

This dreaded threat was discussed by Hitler, as we shall see, at a military conference on 19 May, and on this occasion *'for the first time the movements of German troops in Italy to deal with this eventuality were examined in practical terms'*, going so far as to conclude: *'The Italians cannot be trusted, but on the other hand I am convinced that if a shit storm should happen in Italy, we will get by with relatively small forces, especially since the first advanced combat groups will arrive there within ten days.* It was planned to be able to send a division to Italy with sixty trains a day every two days[33] .

On the same day, 19 May, Ambassador Diekhoff spoke with Spanish Navy Minister Moreno Fernandez, who said he was convinced that the Anglo-Americans, who had an impressive number of ships in the ports of North Africa (800 ships were reported to Hitler), were about to launch an attack on southern Europe soon. And he confirmed that the targets would be Greece and Italy.

The Chief of the 3° Department of the SKL, in giving his appreciation of the situation to Admiral Dönitz on 19 May, also made it known that: *'a report on the planned operations in the Mediterranean based on captured enemy documents. There it is stipulated that both operations are to take place at the same time and that major preparations are also being made in the eastern Mediterranean,* **about which less information has so far been received than in the Algerian sector'.** (bold is the author's)[34] :

In Rome there does not appear to have been the same agitation as in Berlin. The subject of Sicily was broached on 17 May 1943 in a conversation held at Palazzo Venezia with the Duce, in the presence of Ambrosio, Kesselring and von Rintelen (see Document no. 6). It is clear from the conversation that the concern over an enemy landing was not to be found in the targets that the Allies periodically wanted the Italian and German Commands to believe, but that the two essential targets were considered to be Sicily and Sardinia; but there was also concern over the air defence of Italy. No mention was made of an enemy landing in the Morea and Dodecanese. Since the operation was planned with enemy movements departing from Malta and Tunisia, it was clear that

---

32 In his talks in Rome, Admiral Dönitz went to see Mussolini, who said he was concerned that Sicily was *'in great danger'*. The Duce asked that reinforcements for the three German divisions to be sent to Italy include 300 tanks, for three battalions to be transferred 2 to Sardinia, 3 to Sicily, and 1 to southern Italy. They did not discuss the defence of Greece. Dönitz told Mussolini that Hitler also wanted to send the Herman Göring Division and the 7[a] Parachute Division to Italy. On his audience with Victor Emmanuel III, the great admiral told Hitler: *'Warm welcome, giving the impression of a wise and experienced person. The King is animated and lively and has a good memory'.* See, *Visit of the Commander-in-Chief of the Navy to Rome from 12 to 14 May 1943'.* But the next day, 15 May, Victor Emmanuel III wrote in one of his Notes: *'Everything must now be done to keep the country united, and not make rhetorical speeches with only a fascist background. One must maintain close contacts with Hungary, Romania, and Bulgaria, which have little love for the Germans; one should not forget to make possible courtesies to the men of the governments of England and America. One should think very seriously about the possible need to decouple the fate of Italy from that of Germany, whose internal collapse could be as sudden as the collapse of the German Empire in 1918'.*
33 Frederick W. Deakin, *Storia della Repubblica di Salò*, Edizioni Giulio Einaudi, Turin, 1963, p. 346-347.
34 1.Skl 1451/43 gKdos. Chefs.

Sicily appeared the most threatened and therefore represented the enemy's real target. Furthermore, it is clear from the minutes that the Italians insisted on receiving German aid in Sicily, which they had previously refused [accepting only three divisions out of the five that Hitler had proposed to Mussolini to send to Italy], and that this aid, as promised by the Führer, was on its way. Field Marshal Kesselring, who had just returned from a visit to Sicily, reported that the German forces on the island consisted of only three regiments, each of two battalions, but still without artillery, and 56 tanks that were destined for Tunisia, had been held[35].

Operation 'Mincemeat', which had not fooled the top Italian and German military leaders in Rome about a landing in Greece, as the British had hoped, can clearly be defined, due to its uselessness, as a true Operation *Corpse*, and not at all ingenious, because it was predictable, so much so that many senior Allied officers had been opposed to its implementation, which was then authorised, probably to please the British, by General Eisenhower.

But even the Germans were not falling for the British deception. In a '*General Appraisal of the Situation*' compiled by the Seekriegsleitung and dated 20 May 1943, it was stated with regard to the Mediterranean that only North Africa had forces and material for '*a major operation*' to be expected in the western Mediterranean. And it was specified: '*Italy's weakness offers the greatest incentive for an attack on the large Italian islands and mainland Italy with the aim of definitively eliminating Italy from the conflict and building a front in southern Europe in the direction of the Alps*'.

Concerning Greece, although there was some concern about a British plan (Operation 'Mincemeat') to be carried out 'at the same time *as an operation in the western Mediterranean, a landing in Greece with a simultaneous diversionary attack in the Dodecanese*', it was however unequivocally reported: '*At the moment, the **Balkan sector does** not appear to be immediately threatened by landings, reports of the concentration of landing craft and troops in Syria, Palestine and Cyprus not being confirmed so far*[36]'.

▲ The same conviction as Riccardi and Ambrosio was held by the highly intelligent General Mario Roatta, Commander of the Italian 6th Army in Sicily, and later at the time of the landing Chief of Army Staff.

35 ASMEUS, Fund *H* 10, folder no. 10.
36 M. Salewski, *Die deutsche Seekriegsleitung, 1935-1945*, Volume 111: DenkscIniften and Lagebtrachtungen 19, 38 -

▲ Vice Admiral Friedrich Ruge, Commander of the German Navy in Italy was also of the same opinion as the Italian military leadership regarding the safe landing of the Allies in Sicily.

From this it is clear that the SKL's concerns were at this time directed towards the western Mediterranean, and therefore the two pre-eminent targets could only be Sicily and Sardinia. It was to these two islands that the arrival of German reinforcements of men and vehicles was planned.

Another piece of disinformation came from Lisbon, as recorded in a Memo from the Head of the Marita Information Service (SIS) dated 28 May 1943, in which General Cesare Amé, Head of the Military Information Service of the Supreme Command (SIM), described a conversation, deemed reliable, that had taken place between an English personality and a Portuguese, writing:

"The African campaign is over.

The jump to Europe will have to happen without delay.

For this reason, our troops will not be granted long rest. Any delay could be detrimental, given the organisational power of the enemy.
We feel it is necessary to take advantage of the morale factor: the morale of our troops today is very high.
It has never been like this.

How would you make the leap?

It is a secret of the Major States. It will not happen, however, where everyone believes.
We need a large, fixed aircraft carrier in the Mediterranean, to serve as a base for all penetration operations in Europe, which (we are under no illusions) will be costly and hard.

▲ German Ambassador in Madrid, Hans-Heinrich Diekhoff at his residence.

1944, Bernard & Graefe, Frankfurt am Mein, 1973, p. 339-346. Translation by Augusto De Toro.

Sicily?

No. The attack on this island would, for the moment, be a very expensive adventure with no certainty of results. We would first land in Sardinia: this would serve as our aircraft carrier and base for the jump to the south of France.

Even with the conquest of Sardinia, we will free the Mediterranean, which will allow us freedom of movement, which, in spite of everything, we still do not have.

Certainly the resistance will be great and the undertaking is difficult: but we cannot waver in the face of the sacrifices that await us. What matters to us is the final outcome and this we will achieve.

We will begin, I repeat, with Sardinia, for the conquest of which great preparations are being made with the participation of all arms and especially the air force.

Sardinia will be the prelude to the conquest of Europe: in the relevant enterprise, we rely heavily on the enthusiasm of the French troops who are now in North Africa and eagerly waiting to avenge the affront".

On 5 June 1943, at a time when there was supposed to be alarm over the defence of Greece, according to the letters of the fictitious Major Martin, and on the basis of confidential information arriving from Lisbon, Superaereo, the Operational Command of the Regia Aeronautica, made the following assessment of the situation and intentions of the Anglo-Americans (see Document No. 7)[37] :

'The movement of landing craft from west to east passing through the Sicilian Channel could make it appear - in Supermarina's opinion - that Algiers and Tripoli currently constitute backward bases for preparing landing forces for an attack on Sicily. ...

Worthy of note is the increase in the number of landing craft deployed in Bizerte that has occurred continuously over the past three days.

On the basis of the vast amount of information received from secret service agents, trusted persons, interceptions, and aerial reconnaissance, there was no mathematical certainty in Italy as to where the Allies would land in Europe, as there were so many possibilities that starting from Spain they would reach the Dodecanese. In this regard, Colonel Ernest Zolling, who at the time held the position of Chief Information Officer of the OBS, wrote, among other things, in his report of 29 October 1947, which I traced and published in unpublished form in 1980[38] . (For the original form see Document No. 10):

"As far as the *location of the Allied forces was known, at least from a general point of view, one could not venture any predictions as to how the enemy would conduct the war. The Allied Intelligence Service managed to disguise its plans very well at that time. This was achieved not by maintaining absolute secrecy, but instead by propagating a large number of reports about probable landing operations that reached the German Command through various sources, some of which contradicted each other and some of which were confirmed. It was difficult in the large number of reports received to distinguish the probable from the true.*

Spain, southern France, Italy and Greece were repeatedly mentioned as landing targets. A special report of absolute confidence received in mid-May spoke of Sardinia and the Peloponnese [operation 'Mincemeat'].- *Even the concentration of the Allied forces in the centre of the North African coastline did not in itself provide a valid and safe indication for predicting the decisions of the Allied Command. Ultimately, the Algerian and Tunisian ports were the only ports available in the western and central Mediterranean from which any landing operations against the southern European coasts could be launched.*

The OBS considered the landing in the area where it exercised its command, namely the Apennine peninsula

---

37 Archives of the Air Force General Staff Historical Office (henceforth ASMAUS), fonds *M.3*, folder 36.
38 Francesco Mattesini & Alberto Santoni, *La partecipazione tedesca alla guerra aeronavale nel Mediterraneo (1940-1945),* p. 370-371.

and the adjacent islands, to be *likely'*. *This conviction was strengthened by concomitant reports of agents and in mid-June by the conquest of the islands of Pantelleria and Lampedusa (which, however, could be interpreted as a masking action) as well as by the increasingly violent and numerous air attacks by the Allies against the Axis Air Force installations and against the lines of connection and traffic in the Italian area"*.

Thus, in Colonel Zolling's opinion, the landings could have taken place in Italy, Sicily and Sardinia, but not in Greece as the false documents of Operation 'Mincemeat' would have us believe.

From the middle of June, the OBS was convinced that the enemy's landing operation was imminent and since it had to be established with certainty where the blow would be struck, all available means were employed for information purposes: intelligence service, radiotelegraphic interception, aerial reconnaissance and exploration with submarines; measures to which the Allies responded with adequate countermeasures, opposing radiotelegraphic silence and countering the activity of Axis reconnaissance and submarines; but without being able to do anything against the Axis intelligence service in the Gibraltar area, which proved invaluable in signalling the maritime traffic entering the Mediterranean in that focal zone.

On 30 May, Supermarina, which until then had not considered it possible to establish with any certainty whether the Allies would land in Sicily or Sardinia, for the first time, ten days after the start of Operation 'Husky', noted that the deployment of Anglo-American landing craft was directed *'predominantly against Sicily, such that it could be attacked at any time*[39].

▲ Type IV tanks of the 90th Division in Sardinia in the summer of 1943. After the fighting in North Africa, the 90th Light Infantry Division was reconstituted in Sardinia in July as the 90th Panzegrenadier (Armoured Grenadiers).

---

39 Alberto Santoni, *Le operazioni in Sicilia e in Calabria*, USMM, Rome, 1989, p. 53.

CHAPTER 4

GERMAN REINFORCEMENTS IN ITALY

Towards the end of May 1943, Hitler informed Mussolini through the OBS that Germany was ready to provide Italy with five modern divisions for the defence of Italian territory. The Duce enthusiastically received this news; the details were to be discussed the next day with the Supreme Command. But to Field Marshal Kesselring's great surprise, he heard General Ambrosio reply that three divisions were sufficient. The Duce then wrote to Hitler in the same vein. General Ambrosio asked that one of the three divisions be sent to Sicily (where another German division, the 15ª Panzergrenadier, was being formed), another to Sardinia, and a division to southern Italy.

The Hermann Göring Parachute Armoured Division (General Paul Conrath), which had fought in Tunisia and was in reconstitution in the Naples area, was chosen for Sicily, where the 15ª Panzergrenadier Division (General Carl-Hans Lungershausen), also in reconstitution after the African campaign, was already in reconstitution; the 90ª Panzergrenadier Division (General Carl-Hans Lungershausen), which was also in reconstitution after the African campaign, was chosen to move to Sardinia; and the 29ª Panzergrenadier Division (General Walter Fries), which had been destroyed at Stalingrad and had been reconstituted, was chosen to move to Italy from southern France. Later, in June, the two armoured divisions 16ª and 26ª arrived from France, as Hitler had already decided in mid-May, whose movement took place at the same time as the 1ª Armoured Division was sent to Thessaloniki.

The contribution of the German Armed Forces to the defence of Italian territory against an Anglo-American invasion was indeed very opportune at the time. The Italian divisions were in fact very modest, mostly dismounted, with little opportunity for movement and lacking in tanks, heavy artillery and anti-tank guns. Moreover, they were made up of personnel who had received only rough combat training and who, due to many years spent only guarding barracks, depots and coastal positions, had become abulic and with little desire to fight.

The dispatch of considerable German forces to Italy proves that the trick of the fake corpse, regarded with too much exaggeration as the realisation of the greatest hoax of the Second World War (sic), and to make Adolf Hitler convulse, although it had undoubtedly alarmed the Chancellor and Chief of the German Armed Forces and the collaborators of his Headquarters (OKW), it did not, however, contrary to what is often claimed particularly in Britain, mislead the Axis commanders as historians Morison and Roskill have explained; so much so that, during the month of June 1943, numerous German Army reinforcements arrived in Sicily, bringing the Italian-German garrison on the island to 270.0000 men, including 40,000 Germans. In Sardinia there were about 100,000 men, of whom 10,000 were German.

In addition, taking them away from other assignments on the European fronts, two Wing Commands (KG-1 and KG.6) with eight Bombardment Groups, two Fighter Groups, one Wing Command (SKG.10) and three Assault Groups were transferred to Italy (and not to Greece for the protection of the Dodecanese) in the second half of May and early June to reinforce Field Marshal Wolfram von Richthofen's 2ª Air Fleet (2ª Luftflotte.) with as many as eight Bombardment Groups, two Fighter Groups, a Wing Command (SKG.10) and three Assault Groups, which had to be assigned new airfields in the Italian peninsula by the operational body of the Regia Aeronautica General Staff (Superaereo).

By 10 July 1943, the day of the landings in Sicily, the number of combat aircraft of the 2ª Luftflotte had risen to 932, including 40 Ju.88 and Bf.109 reconnaissance aircraft, 356 Ju.88 and Do.217 bombers, 265 Bf.109 fighters, 14 Ju.88 night fighters, 134 FW.190 assault aircraft, 81 Bf.110 and Ju.88 destroyers. To these combat forces, a further 305 aircraft had to be added, stationed at airfields in the eastern Mediterranean (Greece and Crete) under the South-Eastern Command, in particular assigned to the 10th Airborne Corps (Fliegerkorps), which had been taken over from the 2ª Luftflotte. On the Italian side, as of 9 July 1943, 930 combat aircraft were available on the peninsula and islands (including Corsica), while in the Balkans and the Aegean there were a further 210 aircraft, but almost all of them were of modest specification[40].

---

40 Francesco Mattesini and Alberto Santoni, La partecipazione tedesca alla guerra aeronavale nel Mediterraneo (1940-1945), Edizioni dell'Ateneo &Bizzarri, Rome, 1989, p. 379-382. * With regard to attacks against the landing formations,

Both on land and in the air, to which were added as front-line forces for the defence of Sicily submarines and torpedo motorboats (which, contrary to Morison's assertion, were kept at their bases in Augusta and Porto Empedocle), in contrast to the Italians (who could only count on a hundred or so light armoured vehicles of a modest type, Renault R.35 of 10 tons and 37 mm cannon and L.35/33 of 3.5 tons with two machine guns, and as a unit capable of fighting enemy tanks twenty-four self-propelled vehicles, of the 10th Regiment, on M hull with 90/53 guns), the Germans were far better armed and equipped. They had excellent field armament and 110 tanks as part of the Herman Göring Armoured Division (including the 2[a] Company of the 504th Armoured Battalion - s.Pz.Abt.504 - with sixteen Type VI 'Tiger' tanks), and another 60 tanks in the 15[a] Panzergrenadier Division. Both divisions had been continually reinforced to bring them up to their best manpower and means, while four other German divisions (16[a] and 26[a] Panzer, 29[a] Panzergrenadier and 1[a] Parachutist), which were in France for reconstitution, from mid-May were ready for possible action from the south of the Italian peninsula, between Calabria and Basilicata, and another division, the 3[a] Panzergrenadier, was in Tuscany for reconstitution, after having operated on the Russian front[41].

Ultimately, no German forces, as was claimed in order to boast the alleged success of Operation 'Mincemeat', left Sicily for Greece, while during the first half of June, the 1[a] German Armoured Division, under the command of General Walter Krüger, arrived in Greece from Rennes (France) in Thessaloniki.

On the transfer of this division, in order to validate that Operation Mincemeat had been successful, Anglo-Saxon historians attach great importance to it. This is the case of the British Ben Macintyre who rightly reported that the movement of the 1[a] German Armoured Division to Greece had started from France towards the end of May 1943 and was fully operational in June. On this subject Macintyre reported[42] :

"At the end of May, the director of [British] intelligence wrote in his secret naval diary, that "the first German Panzer Division (strength about 18,000 men) was transferred from France to the Thessaloniki region". The information was classified 'A1'. This was the first indication of a major troop movement in response to the Mincemeat documents. An intercepted message added further details of 'arrangements for the passage through Greece to Tripoli in the Peloponnese of the German 1st Panzer Division'. The movement seemed directly related to the information in Nye's letter, and then Tripoli, Montagu noted, was a 'strategic position well adapted to resist our invasion of Kalamata and Cape Araxos'. The First Panzer Division, with eighty-three tanks, had been in fierce action in Russia but was now 'completely reorganised'. Recently spotted by British intelligence in Brittany, the Panzer Division was a formidable, attacking force, and was now being launched from one end of Europe to the other, to counter an illusion".

The question of sending the 1[a] Division to Greece had been discussed and decided on 19 May, during a conversation between Hitler and Field Marshal Keitel, Chief of the OKW, in the presence of General Walter Warlimont, Deputy Chief of Staff of the Wehrmacht, and General Walter Bahle, Chief of Army Staff at the OKW. Hitler argued that because of the threat of an enemy landing in the Peloponnese it was necessary to defend the copper mines in Greece at all costs by sending an armoured division there; but he exclaimed: *'But where to get it'.* Keitel replied: *'All that is available in the West is 24[a] '.* Asked by the Führer how many tanks the 1[a] Armoured Division had, Keitel replied: *'The 1[a] Armoured Division has about 50 tanks ready for deployment'.* Hitler went on to say: *'I have come to the decision to have an armoured division transferred to Greece at all costs, to the Athens area or, better still, directly to the Peloponnese.* But finding an armoured division at that time was not easy. It also turned out that it was very difficult to supply armoured divisions with tanks, so much so that General Warlimont reported that 16[a] , to be transferred to Italy, had only fifty type IV tanks, and 26[a] also to be transferred to Italy 36 type III tanks, with 50 mm long and 75 mm short guns, and three type IVs.

---

in the instructions given to the air force on 28 May 1943 with leaflet 8061/43, Field Marshal Kesselring (OBS) specified: *'It is important that contact be constantly maintained in order to be able to establish in good time where the landings could take place (Sardinia, Sicily, Pantelleria) and to attack these formations with combat aircraft and torpedo bombers.* As can be seen, the areas where landings were possible also included the island of Pantelleria, which the British actually invaded on 10 June, taking possession of its important airport, and the following day also that of Lampedusa. At this point there was no longer any doubt, if not incorrect assumptions, that the Allies' next target would be Sicily.

41 *Ibidem*, 397-398; Alberto Santoni *Le operazioni in Sicilia e in Calabria*, Stato Maggiore dell'Esercito Ufficio Storico, Rome, 1989, p. 48.

42 Ben Macintyre, *Operation Mincemeat. The Nazis and Assured an Allied Victory*, Harmony Books, New York, 2010.

Hitler having asked Warlimont '*Which division do you personally consider the most suitable for immediate deployment in the Balkans*', he was answered '*All things considered, it seems to me that 1ª is the only one ready for deployment*'. And Bahle added that it had 60 Type IV tanks and 12 flame-throwing tanks, but lacked self-propelled artillery. But when it reached its destination, it was calculated that it would be completed '*during the next quarter*'. Finally, considering that the greatest danger to Germany in the event of a landing in Italy or the Balkans was in the Balkans, the decision was taken by the Führer to prepare the 1ª Armoured Division for transfer to Greece. It was also decided to hasten the transfer to Italy of the two armoured divisions 16ª and 26ª, although they were incomplete and were to be completed at their destination, and it was discussed about sending the Luftwaffe Hermann Göring Armoured Division to Sicily, as Hitler wanted to know what his tank situation was (72 including 17 'Tigers' plus 22 StuG III assault guns), because a threat to the west was not to be underestimated[43].

The defence of the Balkans, as well as of Norway, was the obsession of Hitler, who had been pushing the OKW since the autumn of 1942 to convince it to send reinforcements to Greece, including two armoured divisions, the 18ª and the 25ª, later held back for other needs[44]. The Italians, who controlled the Morea and the entire western strip of Greece, had also participated in this reinforcement effort and continued to do so within the limits of available means and armaments.

▲ From left: Field Marshals Albert Kesselring and Wolfram von Richthofen, Commander of the 2nd Luftflotte, visiting the Neptune front in March 1944, discuss the situation. First on the right is General Siegfried Westphal, Chief of Staff of Kesselring's Army Group C.

---

43 Helmut Heiber, *Hitler strategist*, (from the German Deutsche Verlags-Anstalt), Mondadori, Milan 1966, Minutes of 19 May 1943, p. 115-136.
44 British historian Denis Smith writes on page 239 of his book *Deathly Deception* that on 21 May the British cryptographic organisation Ultra, in Bletchley Park (London), deciphered an order to transfer the 1ª Armoured Division from France to Greece. Two days later it learned what the division's strength was, and on 5 June it arrived at its destination in the Balkans on seventy-one trains. No mention is made of the transfer to Italy of six German divisions, armoured and Panzergrenadier, and of the enormous amount of trains needed to transport them. Consequently, Smith concludes, on 8 June, '*a delighted Montagu informed Colonel Bevan of the "Ultra" decryption, because it seemed to prove, beyond doubt, a practical impact of Operation Mincemeat, on the actions of the German High Command*'. Of the subsequent movements of the 1ª armoured division we are not interested. It remained statically in Greece, only to be sent back to the bedlam of the Russian front in the autumn.

Map of Italy showing the locations of the main German units on 25 July 1943, the day of the fall of fascism.

In a memorandum from the Supreme Command to the Duce dated 12 June 1943, with the subject line '*Deployment of Italian and German Forces for the Defence of Greece*', it is reported that the situation of Greece's defensive forces, after the arrival of German reinforcements, was as follows: 8 Italian Divisions; 4 German Divisions, 3 infantry and 1 armoured. Of these German forces, two battalions reinforced the Italian defence of the Corinth Canal; another six fortress battalions were deployed in the Peloponnese in coastal defence or in direct defence of the airfields, from where Italian fighters protected maritime traffic between Italy and Greece[45]. Be that as it may, the sending of the 1ª Armoured Division to Greece did not make that sector any easier compared to what was being reinforced in southern Italy, Sardinia and especially Sicily.

While Mussolini continued to believe that the next Allied landing would take place in Sicily, the gateway to southern Italy, a n d t h e same was the thinking of General Vittorio Ambrosio, Hitler was still convinced that Sardinia was most threatened and, as Frederick W. Deakin wrote, for the following reason[46]:

His interpretation of the future Allied strategy was more coherent than Mussolini's: Hitler foresaw that from Sardinia the enemy would be able to threaten Rome and the main ports of Genoa and Livorno and simultaneously strike all of upper Italy and southern France and from there the heart of the European fortress. The logical consequence of such an Allied move would have been an attempt to outflank the south-eastern flank of the German positions in Europe by means of a large-scale landing in Greece and the Balkans. This, in essence, was Hitler's strategic thinking in those weeks about the war in the Mediterranean and the enemy's upcoming intentions in that area.

The transfer to Sardinia of the 90ª Panzegrenadier Division (General Carl-Hans Lungershaqusen), which took the name 'Division Sardinien', took place in July, as had been promised by Kesselring, for the defence of Sicily and Sardinia; this was followed by the dispatch of the paratroopers of the 1ª Division (1. Fallschirmjäger- Division) of General Kurt Student's XI Fliegerkorps, to be deployed in Calabria[47]. The division was located in France, in the Flers area near Avignon, as part of the reserve of Army Group D.

This urgent reinforcement of the Italian peninsula and islands was certainly due to a report that arrived from Madrid. In fact, on 18 June, the Spanish Foreign Minister, Francisco Gómez-Jordana Sousa, passed the following communication to the German Ambassador in Madrid, which he had learned from the high command of the Spanish General Staff and which Hans-Heinrich Diekhoff immediately transmitted to Berlin in the following form: '*I am informed from a reliable source that the Spanish General Staff received news this evening of important American offensives in the process of being launched from Algeria and Tunis. Probable target, Sicily*[48] '. Three days later, the thought that the Italian Supreme Command brought to Mussolini's attention with the *Appunto al Duce Apprezzamento della situazione alla data del 18 giugno 1943*, which was at that time quite different and much more logical than Hitler's one on Sardinia, because it concerned Sicily at a time when everything led to the belief that it was the Allies' target, claimed[49]:

The enemy has not yet begun air action in preparation for the landing. The bombardments on the airfields and ports of the islands have hitherto had the character of interdiction to prohibit us from using them as a base for air-sea combat in the Strait of Sicily, and therefore today they are on the whole more extensive in Sicily than in Sardinia **precisely for the purpose to which they tend** [the boldface is the author's]. *And the same reasoning explains the dogged action against Messina and Reggio, because the Strait is a vital point for the island's supplies; that is, by bombing the passage, we weaken not only the island's defences but also the offensive capacity of our means against the African bases and the Mediterranean Sea.*

Ultimately, despite what has been said and written, Operation 'Mincemeat' was planned and carried out with undoubted success, but in practice, to the satisfaction of British historians and those abroad who agreed with their thesis, it served no useful purpose in disarming the defence of Sicily and delaying the arrival of reinforce-

45 ASMEUS, *H 9*, folder 6.
46 Frederick W. Deakin, *Storia della Repubblica di Salò*, cit., p. 343.
47 ASMEUS, *Historical Diary of the Supreme Command*, May-July 1943.
48 Frederick W. Deakin, *Storia della Repubblica di Salò*, cit., p. 382.
49 ASMEUS, *L 13*, folder 69.

▲ Panzer VI 'Tiger' tank of the 2ⁿᵈ Company of the 504ᵗʰ Armoured Battalion of the Hermann Göring Armoured Parachute Division in Ragusa, Sicily. The tank weighed 56 tonnes and had an 88 mm cannon.

ments. On the contrary, the Anglo-American preparations for disembarkation, their concentration of landing craft in ports and anchorages stretching from Tripoli to Algeria, their air raids directed above all against the airports and the port of Messina, attacking the ferries in the Straits to diminish Sicily's chances of defence, served to convince even the most sceptical that the enemy's next attack move would concern that island[50].

At the same time, however, the late friend Alberto Santoni wrote, to help the Allies in their work of depredation, there had been:

"undoubtedly a mediocre performance by the Axis Intelligence Services and in this regard it is enough to think that even on 4 July 1943, six days after Operation Husky, the German Secret Service [OKW] believed that simultaneous adversary landings in Sicily, Sardinia and Greece were imminent[51]".

And since the information arriving from the SIM (Military Information Service) was equally mediocre, the Supreme Command and Supermarina were persuaded, at least initially, to take into consideration the idea that the enemy's first target was Sardinia (Sa Exigency), and then argue that in reality the landing could take place in Sicily (Si Exigency), and possibly simultaneously on both islands (SS Exigency)[52].

However, for this last possibility of an enemy landing, in a memorandum of the Supreme Command of 23 June 1943, with the subject *'Occupation of Sicily'*, signed by General Ambrosio, it was reported that the avai-

---

50 The OBS Daily Bulletin No. 1555/25, dated 28 May 1943, which reached Superaereo, states: '*During severe air attacks Messina day 25 sank last viable ferry: therefore rail traffic through Strait of Messina no longer possible at present. Rail traffic continues with small boats'.* See, ASMAUS, DCHG 3/37.

51 Alberto Santoni, *Le operazioni in Sicilia e in Calabria*, cit., p. 49.

52 To add to the confusion, the belief arose that the enemy's landings could also have concerned Provence, in order to threaten Germany from the south with air attacks, or the Balkans to attack the oil installations in Romania, vital for the German and Italian war economy. For all important documents on Si. Sa. and SS operations, see Aurore's book, printed for the Ufficio Storico dell'Aeronautica, *Le direttive tecnico-operative di Superaereo*; Volume II Tomo, *January 1943 - September 1943*, Rome 1992.

lability of Anglo-American landing craft allowed '*sufficient land forces to attempt the invasion of either Sicily or Sardinia, but not both islands at the same time*'. So this last hypothesis, the SS Exigency, was not of much concern[53].

On 24 June 1943, by letter no. 19049 with the subject line "*Appreciation of the situation*", Supermarina informed the Supreme Command and Superaereo that many signs suggested that the Allies had completed their preparations and that the attack would be carried out in an area where maximum air support could be obtained, exploiting the possibilities offered by the airfields of Malta and Pantelleria. It was believed that south-eastern Sicily (from Syracuse to Gela), south-western Sicily (from Gela to Trapani), and southern Sardinia (Gulf of Cagliari) were particularly exposed[54].

On 29 June, on the basis of the enemy's naval deployments that were moving from French North Africa towards the east, and the movements of ships at sea, including battleships and aircraft carriers, Supermarina, with sheet No. 9614, informed the Supreme Command, Super Army, Superaero and OBS. that enemy operations would be directed against targets to the east of Cape Bon, thus certainly in Sicily[55].

At the end of June, the OBS and the Supreme Headquarters were presented with a picture of the situation of the Allied forces evaluated in their overall deployment in North Africa, Gibraltar and Malta at over 780,000 men and 4,000 tanks, to which another 50,000 men were added in Libya. The dislocation of landing craft, according to the OBS assessment, appeared as follows: 6 landing craft in Gibraltar, 238 in the Oran area, 87 in the Bizerte area, 23 in Malta, and 15 in Susa, capable of embarking 34,200 men and 3,110 tanks and vehicles. The location of another 810 landing craft capable of transporting 23,000 men and 400 vehicles remained unknown. These vehicles were probably located in back ports ready to be sent forward in the event of a landing. '*The gathering of Allied forces, land and air, undoubtedly gravitated to the western Mediterranean and aimed at Italy ... the likelihood of landing actions in Sicily*'. This was also confirmed by the presence of a force of about three divisions of paratroopers and airborne troops gathered in the Oran area, in the vicinity of the available airfields in the area[56].

General Alfredo Guzzoni, in one of his orders from Enna, where he commanded the 6ª Army in Sicily, to which the German forces were attached, informed the troops on 30 June of the described situation '*regarding the possibility of enemy landings*'.

On 1 July, with sheet no. 1B/10506, Superaereo sent the Air Force and Air Squadron Commands an '*Appraisal of the Situation*' (see document no. 7), in which, among other things, it warned:

"*Many symptoms suggest that the enemy has completed its preparation and is about to begin the new cycle of operations. The following appreciation can be made of the probable objectives and mode of action:*
1. - It must be assumed that the enemy will operate in areas where they can take advantage of maximum air support.
From this point of view, taking into account the air deployment that, according to the information in our possession, the enemy would have assumed and the possibilities offered by the fields of Malta and Pantelleria, South-eastern Sicily (from Syracuse to Gela), South-western Sicily (from Gela to Trapani) and, to a lesser extent, Southern Sardinia (Gulf of Cagliari) are considered particularly exposed".

On 2 July, the Commander of the 2ª Air Fleet, Field Marshal von Richthofen, in a meeting at the Supreme Command attended by Generals Ambrosio and Fougier and Field Marshal Kesselring, after announcing that the port of Bizerte was saturated with ships and that there were 450 fighter planes on the airfields of Malta and another 50 on Pantelleria, said that these '*will certainly be used by the enemy in support of a landing attempt in Sicily*'[57].

There was now clear evidence of this, such as the intensified bombardment of all targets in Sicily and southern

53 ASMEUS, *Supreme Command Historical Diary*, Annexes, June 1943.
54 AUSMM, *Maristat General Secretariat*, folder 8, file 64.
55 ASMEUS, *M.3*, folder 12.
56 Virgilio Rusca, *O.B.S. logistical and operational organisational problems before the Anglo-American landings in Sicily*, AUSMM.
57 ASMEUS, *M.3*, folder 12.

Italy by the Allied air force, even though it was still believed that the threat could also occur in Sardinia.

On 2 July, the US Magic, the cryptographic service corresponding to the British Ultra, intercepted and decrypted a report from the Japanese ambassador in Rome, in which he made various assumptions in the Italian capital about the Allies' intentions. Interestingly, point C) of the report states: '*It is generally believed that landings will be made in Sicily and Sardinia. There is irrefutable evidence that, efforts are being made to disrupt communications in these areas*[58] '.

On this subject, in a report dated January 1948, entitled '*The air situation in the western and central Mediterranean from the loss of Tunisia to the landing in Sicily. Structure and employment of the 2nd Air Fleet at that time*' (see Document No. 10), Air Squadron General Paul Deichmann, then Chief of Staff of the OBS, wrote[59]:

"*When at the beginning of June the attacks were concentrated against the airports in Sicily and at the end of June against the ferries serving the Strait, so that of five only one was still in service, it appeared that Sicily was to be the territory chosen for the next landing.*

While the Allied twin-engines, which more or less corresponded to the German twin-engines, limited their attacks to coastal targets, the four-engines conducted their destructive attacks against any target throughout Italian territory.

These four-engine attacks were of great importance, because they succeeded in breaking the Italian unity for the further conduct of the war. Their successes were decisive for Italy's subsequent exit from the Axis.

An Allied four-engine attack almost resulted in the death of the O.B.S., Field Marshal Kesselring. During one of his visits to Marsala, the house in which he was staying was destroyed and two staff officers from his retinue were killed".

By now there was no longer any doubt about the action's prediction and its target of Sicily, '*although the OKW, which by then no longer cared about Greece, insisted on considering the possibility of a simultaneous landing in Sicily and Sardinia*[60] '.

Sicily was the target that the Allies, with the deception of Operation 'Mincemeat', wanted to hide until the landing, without succeeding. And the landing began on the night between 9 and 10 July, when by then, with the reinforcements that had arrived during the month of June, there was a garrison of 270,000 men on the island, of whom about 40,000 were Germans (from the 10,000 who were there when the false Major Martin was found on the beach at Huelva), with 160 tanks, part of the Herman Göring Armoured Division and the 15a Panzergrenadier Division. That is to say, the number of German soldiers, who according to the Operation Mincemeat plan were to move from Sicily to reinforce Greece, had quadrupled and considerably armed. Even the rest of the German troops in Italy, four divisions, two of which were armoured, were not moved beyond the peninsula from their deployment locations in Tuscany, Calabria and Apulia. In addition, as General Frido von Senger und Etterlin, liaison officer to the Command of the Italian 6a Army[61] in Sicily commanded by General Alfredo Guzzoni, wrote after the war, there were another 30,000 men on the island, on the German side, '*as anti-aircraft defence troops, Luftwaffe ground personnel, subsistence units and so on*'. Therefore, the German garrison in Sicily was already very strong because, while little could be done with the men of the various services, the thirty-three anti-aircraft artillery batteries with 88 mm guns could be used as deadly anti-tank weapons.

The Allies' knowledge of German reinforcements in Sicily was kept under constant observation by the British cryptographic organisation Ultra, and other sources of information. In the third week of May 1943, the Anglo-Americans learned that the German troops already in Sicily had acquired divisional status, with headquarters in Caltanissetta in the centre of the island, and that these forces were being reorganised into a Panzer Grenadier Division, with three regiments, one of which was retained to reinforce a particular point on the coast. Between 20 June and early July, decryptions warned of the arrival of the Hermann Göring Division with

58 U.S National Archives, Washington D.C., document S.R.S. 1221. Quoted by Alberto Santoni in *Le operazioni in Sicilia e in Calabria*, USMM, Rome, 1989, p. 55.

59 Virgilio Rusca, *O.B.S. logistical and operational organisational problems before the Anglo-American landings in Sicily*, AUSMM.

60 *Ibid.*

61 Frido von Singer und Etterlin , *Krieg in Europa*, translated into Italian *Combattere senza paura e senza speranza*. Longanesi, Milan, 1968, p. 207.

18,000 men, 96 guns and 53 tanks, but without its third infantry regiment. On 8 July (D-Day 2 of Operation 'Husky'), the intelligence service learned that the Division formed in Sicily, had been renamed 15ª Panzerdivision, and had transferred its company of about 15 Tiger tanks to the Hermann Göring Division. At the same time, it became known that the Italians had six divisions in Sicily as part of the 6ª Army, and that they were continuously reinforced with weapons and equipment brought in from the peninsula[62].

The final proof of the landing in progress was received on 9 July, when a German scout received news that it was in contact with the Allied landing fleet heading from Malta towards southern Sicily.

As for Operation 'Mincemeat', the British work on Ultra decryptions, after noting considerable German anxiety about an Allied threat to Greece, with particular regard to the Peloponnese, realised on 27 June that operationally 'Mincemeat' had been useless. On that day, an order from Field Marshal Kesselring was deciphered, informing the German forces in the Mediterranean, *'that the hour of decision was at hand and it was necessary to be ready to protect the homeland on Italian soil'*. The intercepted message showed that an Allied attack on Sardinia or the Italian peninsula was now to be ruled out, and that the attention of the Axis forces was turned exclusively to the defence of Sicily, which was now considered to be *'the most likely Allied target*[63]'.

---

62 Hinsley F.H. et al, *British Intelligence in the Second World* War, Volume 3, Part 1, HMSO, London, 1984, p.75 - 76.
63 *Ibid*, p. 79.

▲ In this image from the summer of 1942 in Russia, General Wolfram Karl Ludwig Moritz Hermann Freiherr von Richthofen, then Commander of the 8th Airborne Corps (8th Fliegerkorps) and, from spring 1943, Field Marshal Commander in Italy of the 2nd Airborne Fleet (Luftflotte 2), talks with Field Marshal Alexander Löhr, Commander of the 4th Luftflotte, to which the 8th Fliegerkorps belonged.

▼ LST tank landing craft, loaded to the hilt with men and trucks, in a convoy bound for Sicily.

CHAPTER 5

WHY THE LANDING OF THE ALLIES WAS EXPECTED

Field Marshal Kesselring, well served in the intelligence field by his excellent aerial reconnaissance, and sharing the opinions of the Italians, believed that the primary objective of the Anglo-Americans' next move favoured Sicily, also because the concentration of their hundreds of landing craft to carry out the enterprise was in the area between Bizerte and Tripoli, and the dislocation of troops between Oran and Malta[64]. The same could be said for the concentration of aviation, where the mass of Anglo-American fighter aircraft to support the landing was reported to be concentrated in the airfields and airstrips of north-east Tunisia and Malta, to which Pantelleria was added. In addition, at the beginning of June, the air offensive by the Allies, which until then had involved the uninterrupted attack on targets at every point of Italian territory (ports, airports, railway junctions, factories), was concentrated against the airports in Sicily and at the end of the month on the ferries serving the Strait of Messina, from which supplies and reinforcements flowed[65].

For the same obvious reasons, that the enemy landing would take place in Sicily, Mussolini and Ambrosio were more and more convinced of this, and reading the documents of the exact same idea, in the end, albeit with some distinctions regarding Sardinia, so were the Chiefs of Staff of the Army (General Mario Roatta), the Navy (Admiral Arturo Riccardi) and the Air Force (General Rino Corso Fougier). The latter took the only S.79 torpedo bomber group available there, the 104th, out of the Dodecanese in May, bringing it back to Italy. Had there been an eloquent concern for the Aegean Possession or Greece, with enemy naval movements set in motion in the eastern Mediterranean, that unit would have remained in Rhodes.

Taking these realities into account, which was then shared by the Italian Supreme Command[66], finally allowed the OBS to make fairly accurate predictions of enemy intentions regarding the landing. In fact, by linking the news of the reconnaissance with those communicated by agents in enemy territories, which, among other things, indicated the presence in Malta of three battalions of paratroopers and a commando unit, the OBS finally had confirmation that the next Allied objective would be Sicily. This hypothesis was also favoured by the experience of the always prudent and methodical conduct of the war by the Anglo-Americans who, in order to carry out such a feat, could have had the large airfields of Tunisia and Malta close enough to guarantee constant air support, which would instead have been only partially possible by carrying out a landing in the Morea or the Dodecanese.

Sicily was the only obstacle that would have prevented the Allies from disembarking in the Italian peninsula through the Strait of Messina, while Sardinia, in the opinion of the OBS, from an operational point of view, as we have said, could not give great advantages since its eventual conquest, contrary to Hitler's opinion, would not have brought the Allies any closer to southern Italy, and at the same time, as the then Chief of Staff of the Regia Aeronautica, General Giuseppe Santoro, pointed out 'The *loss of Sicily would have had the very serious consequence of no longer allowing communications with the eastern Mediterranean; which would have had incalculable repercussions on supplies to the Greek chessboard*[67]'.

A simultaneous landing in Sicily and Sardinia was ruled out by the OBS because, in the opinion of Kesselring, who apart from his usual optimism was a true strategist with whom the Allies would have to contend in the Italian campaign of 1943-1945, from an operational point of view it would have entailed the use of substantial

---

64 Francesco Mattesini (Mario Cermelli proofreading), *Le direttive tecnico-operative di Superaereo*; Volume Two II Tomo, *January 1943 - September 1943*, Stato Maggiore dell'Aeronautica Ufficio Storico, Rome, 1992, Various documents, including the set of defence plans of the three Italian Armed Forces and the OBS for the "*Sardinia, Sicily and SS*".
65 Francesco Mattesini and Alberto Santoni, La partecipazione tedesca alla guerra aeronavale nel Mediterraneo (1940-1945), cit. p. 387.
66 On 25 May, General Fougier transmitted to the Office of the R.A. General at OBS, Wenceslas D'Aurelio, the following message No. 1B/8975 to be brought to the attention of Field Marshal Kesselring: "*Supreme Command habet ordered offensive actions on Malta with the task of counter-preparing the adversary landing preparations. Such actions should be conducted in accordance with OBS.*" Attacking the targets of Malta, whose air defences were formidable, meant that the Supreme Command believed that the threat of landings concerned Sicily.
67 Giuseppe Santoro, *L'Aeronautica Italiana nella seconda guerra mondiale*, Volume Secondo, Edizioni esse, Milan - Rome, 1957, p. 530.

▲ The *Howe*, Britain's most modern battleship, moved to the Mediterranean along with its sister ship King George V to support the Sicily landings.

naval means, which the Allies were not believed to possess. But the most important and convincing cause was, according to Kesselring, the fact, discussed at various meetings, that the conquest of Sicily would end up having strong repercussions on the morale of the Italian people and also of its ruling class, with greater effects than would have been produced by the eventual loss of Sardinia[68] . These were logical calculations, and it is not clear why instead the British had organised a staging that a priori was destined to have no effect on German and Italian defensive intentions[69].

But the sure proof that the landing was imminent came in the last week of June and the beginning of July, when the intelligence service reported the passage through the Strait of Gibraltar, heading for the western Mediterranean, of six large British units, four battleships (*Howe, King George V, Warspite, Valiant* joining the *Nelson* and the *Rodney*) and two aircraft carriers (*Formidable* and *Indomitable*), followed by several hospital ships at short distance from each other. This confirmed the imminence of the action, which was also corroborated by the news from trusted agents in North Africa about the eastward movement of troops, landing craft and transport ships to Algeria and Tunisia[70].

68 Regarding the question of the defence of Sicily, Sardinia, central Italy and Corsica, numerous meetings between the Italian and German authorities took place at the Supreme Command, and on these occasions the Italians insistently requested that Germany supply large quantities of modern weapons, such as planes, tanks, anti-aircraft and anti-tank guns, vehicles and fuel for the Navy and Air Force, requests which the Supreme Command then sent to the OKW in a detailed note of 2 May 1943. These requests, which were also supported by those made at the same time by the OBS, were accepted by Germany as far as possible. And it could do no more as it had to protect the coastlines of almost the whole of Europe, as well as fighting a war for life against the Soviet Union.

69 *Ibid*, p. 393. * At a meeting on 1 June 1943 held at the Supreme Headquarters, attended by General Ambrosio and on the German side by Field Marshal Kesselring and Generals von Rintelen and Siegfried Westphal (Chief of Staff of the OBS), Kesselring said: '*I have seen the troops of the "Baade" Division* [actually Colonel "Baade"'s Group, on which the possible employment of local German troops depended] *and the other German troops in Sicily. In eight days the training will be completed and the troops will be ready for deployment. ... As armament we are still missing some of the vehicles...*'. No reference to the imaginary landing in the Morea, as evidently the climate had already changed by then. See, SMEUS, *Minutes of the Meetings held by the Chief of the General Staff*, Volume IV, Rome 1985, p. 150.

70 Participating in the first phase of the landing, which took place over a coastline of 80 miles (130 kilometres), and thus larger than the Normandy invasion, were 2,590 ships of all types (of which 1,614 British, 945 American and 31 from other Allied navies), embarking seven divisions with a total of 181,000 men, of which 115,000 were British and 66,000 American, as well as 14,000 vehicles, 600 tanks and 1,800 guns. The Anglo-American air force fielded a total of 3,445 aircraft, of which 2,510 were operational as of 10 July 1943.

All this served to confirm to the OBS that the landing in Sicily was to be expected at any moment, and that according to the meteorologists, the period between 1 and 10 July would be the most probable due to the moonless night that would facilitate the approach of the landing craft to the coast in favourable conditions, as in fact happened.

On 4 July, in the appreciation of the situation formulated by the Strategic Reconnaissance Committee, attended by representatives of the Italian and German aviation forces at Supermarina's campaign headquarters in Santa Rosa, it was noted that the deployment of the Alerts' air forces was directed against Sardinia and Sicily, while there did not appear to be sufficient air forces to support a major operation in the eastern Mediterranean, which excluded Greece (see Document No. 8).

When, on 6 July, the Anglo-American air force began a formidable pounding against Sicily, Calabria and Puglia, with direct action on airports, commands, traffic centres and other military targets such as troop and vehicle concentrations, coastal fortifications, supply depots and ferries in the Strait of Messina, the OBS no longer had any doubts about the landing and its objective. Disagreeing with the OKW, which insisted on considering the possibility of a simultaneous landing in Sicily and Sardinia, the OBS considered that Sicily was the enemy's chosen point and consequently transhipped part of its last available reserves to the island from Calabria in an attempt to provide the Italians with more support.

The next day, 7 July, Supermarina informed all the Naval Commands, warning them (see Document No. 9):

"It is believed that the enemy is ready to begin landing operations in Sicily and possibly with a diversionary character in Sardinia alt Beginning of these operations depends on carrying out preparatory air phase whose duration is not foreseeable but which could also be very short".

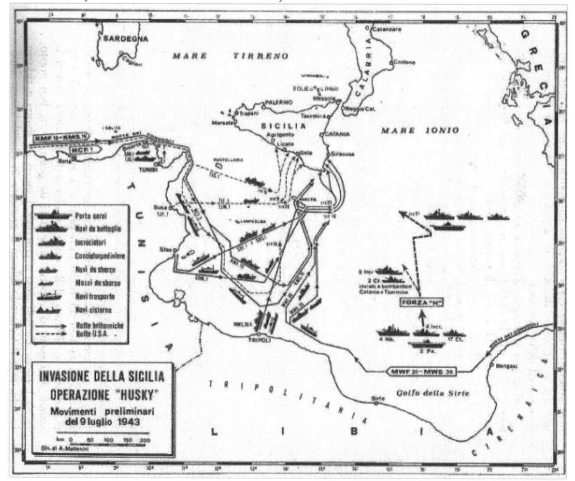

▲ Map drawn by the author's father, Antonio Mattesini.

In the final analysis, no German land, naval or air units left for Greece or anywhere else in Sicily, which on the contrary was considerably reinforced, rendering the attempt of Operation Mincemeat, whose main purpose was precisely that no reinforcements would arrive there, in vain. This is an indisputable fact.

It is hard to see how the corpse of Glyndwr Michael '*could have changed the fate of the Second World War*', which is still the current opinion in many quarters. And the 1956 film *The Man Who Never Was*, starring the great American actor Clifton Webb in the part of the main perpetrator of the 'Mincemeat' plan, Commander Ewen Montagu, who wrote about the episode in a book from which the film was made, is to be regarded as a real historical fact which, we repeat, despite what is believed in Great Britain (and also in Italy), had no practical result. It did, however, serve to bring Montagu, improvised writer and scriptwriter, fame and a lot of money. Other than '*the deception that changed human history*', as it is written on an Italian website. I wonder if by describing historical episodes, blinded by hatred for Nazis and fascists, one can be more naïve and clueless.

One can make the most varied considerations and objections, but one fact is certain, not nonsense. Among the hundreds of documents I consulted, in the end the majority of the opinions of the Major States on where the Anglo-Americans would land always led to one conclusion: Sicily. And it was Sicily rather than Sardinia that was, within the limits of possibility, continually reinforced by the Italians and Germans, who did not fail to prepare action plans for both islands. They also provided for the intervention of the Italian fleet, particularly recommended by Berlin and the OBS; and the latter undertook to ensure the indispensable air escort with its fighter squadrons. As is well known, the Italian ships, angering the Germans, did not intervene because the gap in the Allies' naval forces supporting the landing in Sicily was too great. It appears that even Mussolini was aware of this, and since the navy could only deploy two battleships and five cruisers against the enemy, which were available at the time, as an intelligent person he made no opposition when he was informed by Admiral Riccardi on 10 July.

A summary of the events leading up to the landing in Sicily in the period 1 July - 10 July, compiled by Supermarina, can be found in Document No. 11.

▲ The gravestone on Martin's grave in the cemetery of Huelva. From Wikipedia. Initially it read: '*William Martin, born 29 March 1907, died 24 April 1943, the beloved son of John Glyndwyr Martin and Antonia Martin of Cardiff, Wales*'. In 1998 the British government revealed Michael's true identity, and today the modified plaque reads: '*Glyndwyr Michael; serving in the Royal Marines as William Martin with the rank of Major*'.

CHAPTER 6

THE IRRITATION OF GERMAN FOREIGN MINISTER JOACHIM VON RIBBENTROP

After the Allies had landed in Sicily, Germany's Foreign Minister, Joachim von Ribbentrop, immediately realised that the highly secret information he had received from Spain on 12 May 1943 about the Allies' plans in the Mediterranean, which concerned Greece and the Peloponnese and excluded a landing in Sicily, had been a well-conceived fabrication by the enemy. Therefore, on 29 July, he sent a rebuke to Ambassador Diekhoff in Madrid, accusing him of not having been particularly attentive to the information passed to him that was a forgery attributed 'to the possibility of Spanish complicity in the whole operation'.

Feeling accused of negligence by his superior, Diekhoff, and having the utmost confidence in the Spaniards who had passed on the information to him, he replied that in handing over the documents, by Foreign Minister Jordana and Foreign Ministry Secretary José Maria Doussinague, and later discussing them with Naval Minister Agustín Muñoz Grandes, no one wanted to mislead Germany about the news, since the documents had also been checked by German counter-intelligence 'without a shadow of doubt being cast on their authenticity'. Moreover, the information received by Foreign Minister Jordana on 15 June, and learned from the High Command of the Spanish General Staff, was significant, because it made it known that the enemy was preparing to launch an attack from French North Africa, with Sicily as its probable target.

Undeterred, von Ribbentrop dwelled on the fact that the documents reported 'that only a feint was planned against Sicily ... whereas instead the main attack was launched against Sicily'. This led to the conclusion, he concluded, that the British documents had been fabricated 'for the purpose of causing Sicily to take no defensive measures, or insufficient measures ..., and it was necessary to know whether indeed 'the British deliberately fabricated these documents and procured that they should fall into Spanish hands so that they might reach us by the wrong means. It only remains to be seen whether the Spaniards, realising the game, scientifically lured us onto a false trail or whether they too were played by the Intelligence Service'.

Diekhoff, reiterating that he had full confidence in those who had passed the information on to him, replied that 'those who had spoken to him about the documents and noted their importance, such as the Spanish General Staff, who notified our Abweher of them, also evidently placed full faith in them'.

Diekhoff was convinced that the plans were true, and that they had been changed by the Anglo-Americans when they realised that they had fallen into the hands of the Spanish, choosing Sicily as their other target. Ribbentrop, evidently irritated, had one of his subordinates respond, but remained convinced that it had been a British manipulation of deception.

However, in spite of the state of humiliation in Berlin when they realised that they had been deceived by British Intelligence, the importance of this whole story is that the British did not gain any advantage, because the Italians and the O.B.S. did not fall for the trap, and in June and early July 1943 the reinforcement of Sicily was carried out according to what had been planned for the defence of the island. And the landing did not come unexpectedly[71].

***

In conclusion. The errors that are to be credited to Montegu and the British Intelligence Service's belief in the complete success of Operation Mincemeat have been reported in articles published by Professor Klaus-Jurgen Muller, and can be shared[72].

Noting that the written arguments about the final results of the Mincemeat were detailed and factual enough to initially convince Hitler and the operational staff of the OKW, Muller argued that it was not sufficient to report the military movements of German forces as the cause of the Mincemeat without detailed research in the Germanic archives, which showed that some of the troop movements had already been decided upon earlier by the OKW.

---

71 Frederick W. Deakin, *Storia della Repubblica di Salò*, cit., p. 381-383.
72 *A German Perspective on Allied Deception Operations in the Second World War* and *Intelligence and National Security*.

Some of the other movements that Montegu assumed were a response to Mincemeat were not; the knowledge of the dispatch of the 1ª Armoured Division to Greece was correct, but not that of Field Marshal Erwin Rommel's transfer to Greece to take over command of the German forces, as in fact that assignment was received on 23 July as a result of Operation 'Animals'; that is, the activity of the British SOE in organising sabotage by the Greek resistance.

Some of the alleged battle orders cited by Montegu and British Intelligence were wrong. Hitler's and the OKW's main strategic concern was not so much the expected likelihood of the Allies landing in Sicily, but the collapse of Italy or defection to the Allies, and securing the Balkans, which is why even before the 'Mincemeat' the Germans had agreed with the Italians to reinforce their positions in Greece, Crete and the Dodecanese.

Wrong is the notion that, because of the 'Mincemeat', the defence of Sicily had been shifted eastwards and northwards (to Sardinia), and that until 12 July, three days after the landings, there was a belief in the Axis that this was a diversion. Even a German mine barrage implemented on 20 May on the coast of Greece, together with an increase in coastal defence, were elements that had already been planned by the Italians and Germans; and equally erroneous is the assertion that a German tank force had been sent to Corsica, since this measure too had already been decided before the 'Mincemeat', agreeing with the Italians to transfer the 'SS Reichsführer' assault brigade to reinforce the island's defences.

Initially, as it appears from a conversation with the Duce on 17 April 1943, with Field Marshal Marshal Kesselring and Colonel Ernest-Gunter Baade, in charge of overseeing the organisation of the German troops in Sicily, Mussolini was informed that the "SS Reichsführer" Assault Brigade was already on its way to Sardinia, except that it was to be sent to Corsica, as the 90ª Panzergrenadier Division would be sent to Sardinia[73] . Thus, the displacement of the Assault Brigade was not a consequence of the 'Mincemeat' documents, since its arrival in Italy had begun long before.

It does not appear from the documents that German naval units (torpedo boats) had left Italian ports to move to the Aegean, but only carried out movements involving the escorting of sea convoys in the Tyrrhenian Sea and between Italy and the Aegean.

Finally, something ridiculous. It was written that through an interception of the GC&CS (Government Communications Headquarters), on 9 July, four hours before the landing, the Germans had reinforced the Sardinian forces with twenty-one planes. The displacement of the planes did not concern the protection of Sicily, since in early June 1943, all Italian and German bombing forces had been transferred from Sicily and Sardinia to airfields in Italy, in particular to airfields in Apulia, to save them from destructive attacks by the Anglo-American air force. The twenty-one aircraft had been transferred to Sardinia for the sole purpose of being able to attack, at a decisive moment of the landing in Sicily, the Allied invasion convoys moving along the coasts of Algeria and Tunisia. These actions took place continuously with even very large bomber formations, targeting the landing craft in the ports of Bizerte, Bona, Philippeville, etc. Once the operation had been carried out, the aircraft returned from Sardinia to their bases in peninsular Italy[74].

From all these considerations, we completely disagree with what British historian Denis Smith wrote in the preface to one of his books, namely that: "*through a corpse*", of an operation, the Mincemeat, which brought virtually no strategic or tactical results, "*had been imaginatively and ingeniously and audaciously executed ... one of the most complex stratagems ever attempted in the annals of* war"[75].

It follows that the Allies had not achieved any tactical surprise, because already for almost three weeks, that is, at least from the beginning of the third week of June to 10 July 1943, the Italians and Germans had been certain that the landing would take place in Sicily, where the defensive deployments, with reinforcements already arrived, had been implemented, with the decision for a mobile defence inland rather than a static defence of the beaches. Unfortunately, more reinforcements of men and means, already available in Italy, could have arrived, but this was prevented by the lack of naval means of transport in the Straits of Messina, and by the difficulty of travelling by land along the winding roads and the uncomfortable railways of Campania and Ca-

73 SMEUS, *Diario Storico del Comando Supremo*, Volume IX (1.1.1943-30.4.1943), Tomo II, *Allegati*, Rome, 2000, p. 353-354.

74 Francesco Mattesini, *Gli aerosiluranti italiani e tedeschi nella seconda guerra mondiale (1940-1945). Successes and Disappointments*, Volume 1 and 2, Luca Cristini Editore, Zanica (BG), October 2022. See also, Francesco Mattesini, *Gli aerosiluranti italiani e tedeschi nella seconda guerra mondiale (1940-1945). Successes and Disappointments*, Volume 1 and 2, Luca Cristini Editore, Zanica (BG), October 2022.

75 Smith Denis, *Deathly Deception*, Oxford University Press, 2010.

▲ The Foreign Minister of the Third Reich: Joachim von Ribbentrop. Bundesarchiv.

▲ Spanish Navy Minister Agustín Muñoz Grandes, here in German uniform, and around his neck the Knight's Cross.

labria, which were interrupted in several places by Allied air attacks. There was also the lack of railway tanks to transport combat vehicles and troops, because they were engaged in military services throughout Europe. Finally Hitler, who did not lack intelligence, after an initial moment in which he believed that Major Martin's documents, consulted by experts and widely discussed, were true, on 18 May, having received a report on the increase in US strategic air force activity against Sicily, had a doubt, and speaking to Luftwaffe General Eckhard Christian asked, referring to Martin's corpse: '*This body could not be a deception*'.

It is also good to know what the availability of German forces in Greece and the Aegean was at the time of the Sicily landings. On the Italian side, there were eight Infantry Divisions of the 11ª Army (General Carlo Vecchiarelli) in Greece, three of which were considered efficient; on the German side, there were four Divisions, of which 11ª Infantry Division, 104ª and 117ª Hunters Division (Alpini), and 1ª Armoured Division, the only one with armed tanks; in Crete, the 22ª German Infantry Division, and in Rhodes, the motorised SS 'Rhodos' Brigade. In Italy, there were the Hermann Göring and 15ª Panzergrenadier Divisions (in Sicily), the 16ª and 26ª Armoured Division, the 29ª Panzergrenadier Division, joined by the 3ª Panzergrenadier Division, withdrawn from the Russian front, and the 1ª Parachute Division. In Sardinia was the 90ª Panzergrenadier Division and in Corsica the 'SS Reichsführer' Assault Brigade.

Thus, it is hard to see why, according to the estimators of Operation Mincemeat, the 1ª Armoured Division, on its way to Greece, considered vital to Germany, would be diverted from reinforcements for Sicily. There were sufficient German forces in Italy to intervene in Sicily, but the greatest difficulties, as we have explained, were in getting them to the island due to the lack of naval means, which constituted one of the main objectives of the Anglo-American air force, and one of the Allies' trump cards. After the landing on 10 July, the 29ª Panzergrenadier Division was able to cross the Straits of Messina, and half of the 1ª Parachute Division was transferred to Sicily by air, with heavy losses caused by the attacks of the Anglo-American fighters.

Poor intelligence or misinformation? Or, I am sure, trying at all costs to make Operation 'Mincemeat' appear to be a British intelligence success, which in reality was a crushing failure of deception? From what Roskill, Playfair and Liddle Hart, not to mention Morison, have written, it appears that they were quite upset about the alleged success of Operation 'Mincemeat', pointing out that the Italian and German Commands and intelligence services had been more adept at figuring out what the objective of the landing was, (and thus also the deception of Greece).

***

A final consideration. Regarding the identification of Sicily as the target for the Allied landing in the Mediterranean, the Military Information Service of the Italian Supreme Command (SIM) had been convinced of this since 13 February 1943, believing that after the conquest of Tunisia the Allies would land on the island[76]. Neither did the many false reports that were artfully reported by the Anglo-American intelligence services and news from neutral nations favourable to them, where there were a number of agents whose task was to carry out misdirection and confusion with regard to Germany and Italy, suggest otherwise.

General Cesare Amè, Head of the SIM, referring to the '*false documents placed on a corpse dressed as a British officer and abandoned at sea*', which, according to a British publication, created confusion and misapprehensions and forced the suspension of the work to defend Sicily, argued that these considerations were '*entirely imaginary*'. And he concluded by stating: '*The false documents written in the hand of the British Deputy Chief of the Imperial H.M.S.*', did not serve the purpose of misdirection, but instead made the SIM confirm '*the exact assessment*', i.e. that the target of the enemy landing was indeed Sicily[77].

It was, as we have said, also the consideration of Winston Churchill, who evidently, leaving it to General Eisenhower to authorise the feasibility of Operation 'Mincemeat', believed that Italians and Germans, '*all but one damned fool*' (Adolf Hitler), would not fall into Ewen Montegu's trap.

---

76 Even Captain of the frigate Mario De Monte, Head of Service Office 'B', on which the Foreign Interception and Cryptographers' Services of the Regia Marina's 5th Secret Information Department (SIS) depended, wrote in one of his post-war books that, among the many reports received on Anglo-American operations, '*the most likely hypothesis was that of a landing in Sicily*', which 'had been *planned for some time*'. See, Mario De Monte, *Uomini ombra, Ricordi di un addetto al Servizio Segreto Navale*, Nuova edizione marinara italiana, Rome, 1955, p. 227.

77 Cesare Amè, *Guerra Segreta in Italia 1940 - 1943*, Gherardo Casini Editore, Rome,1954 p. 137).

Today we know that the populists are the ones who, by making films and writing novels and articles on the subject, fuelled the supposed success of an operation, the Mincemeat, that absolutely did not work.

Ultimately, the deluded are still in the United Kingdom today, and the naive, the product of ignorance, among all those who, particularly in Italy, believed in and glorified that macabre staging.

Fortunately on the British side we have an excellent summary of the Sicilian campaign by Liddell Hart, who wrote[78] :

"*Two months passed before the Allies, taking advantage of the victory achieved in Tunisia, landed in Sicily on 10 July. Even then, to meet the attack of eight Allied divisions, there were only two German divisions on the island [the six Italian divisions, except for a few artillery regiments, had disbanded with a shameful 'all at home']. But the Germans, despite lacking air support and receiving only two reinforcement divisions, managed to contain the invading army, which had received far greater reinforcements. After delaying the advance of the Allied armies until mid-August, the Germans evaded the hunt by retreating through the Straits of Messina thanks to effective anti-aircraft protection. Field Marshal Kesselring, commander-in-chief of the German forces in southern Italy, was delighted with the respite provided by the German troops in Sicily; but he also found considerable relief when they repaired safe and sound to Calabria because he had feared that the adversary, with a landing on the tip of the Italian boot, might block their retreat while they were still engaged in Sicily*".

This was the outcome of the Sicilian campaign, in which Operation 'Mincemeat' had no influence.

▲ Another image of Joan Leslie, the young secretary working in Lieutenant Commander Montagu's office, promoted to fiancée of the man who never was...

---

78 B.H. Liddell Hart, *History of a Defeat. Parlano i generali del III Reich*, Rizzoli, Milan, 1973 (3ᵃ edition), p. 385.

DOCUMENTS

MILITARY ATTACHÉ OFFICE BERLIN

INCOMING TELEGRAM

For encrypted teletype

From Supreme Command

Left on 13 May 1943 at 01.35 hours
Arrived 13 May 1943 at 03.00 hours

(*Text*)

No. 12959/Op. prot. high *Pope*

The following telegram from the DUCE is sent with the request that it be sent to the Führer alt. as soon as possible

"Führer, the situation in the Mediterranean puts the defence of the Italian islands in the foreground, possession of which would give the enemy great possibilities on the entire southern European front alt to strengthen that defence, we need more than troops, vehicles of which, as you know, we are in short supply alt I thank you for your offer to send five divisions, but I consider it sufficient to limit them to three to be stationed respectively in Sardinia in Sicily These divisions, like all the other German units already in Italy, will be attached to the Italian commands with territorial and tactical jurisdiction. alt In addition to the above three divisions, I repeat the need for the urgent dispatch of at least thirty bombing squadrons; of fifty 88 mm batteries of six tank battalions (three for Sicily, two for Sardinia and one for Corsica) minimum necessary to set up the defence of the islands alt
Since there is no time for training, these departments should be granted the relevant personnel alt With the end of the operations in Africa and since the German troops on Italian territory came under the Army General Staff, the Führungabteiilung returned to the O.B.S. and a liaison body was created between the O.B.S. and the Royal Army General Staff alt

Receive Führer my ever-cameratical greetings alt Mussolini'.

Order General Silvio Rossi
(23301205)

This letter addressed to General Sir Harold Alexander was dated 23 April 1943.

Personal and Secret

My dear Alex,

I would like to take this opportunity to send you a personal handwritten letter from one of Mountbatten's officers, to give you the inside story of our recent exchange of cables about operations in the Mediterranean and related cover plans. You may have thought that our decisions were somewhat arbitrary, but I can assure you that the C.O.S. Committee gave the utmost consideration to both your and Jumbo's recommendations.

We had recent information that the Boche [Germans] had strengthened and reinforced their defences in Greece and Crete and C.I.C.S. felt that our forces for the assault were insufficient. It was agreed by the chiefs of staff that the 5^a division should be reinforced by a group of brigades for the assault on the beach south of Cape Araxos and that a similar reinforcement should be made for the 56^a division at Kalamata. We are allocating the necessary forces and dispatches.

Jumbo Wilson had proposed selecting Sicily as the cover target for 'HUSKY'; but we have already chosen it as the cover for 'BRIMSTONE'. The C.O.S. Committee took up the whole matter in detail and came to the conclusion that, in view of the preparations in Algeria, the amphibious training that will take place on the Tunisian coast and the heavy aerial bombardment that will be suppressed to neutralise the Sicilian airfields, we should stick to our plan of making "BRIMSTONE" cover - in fact, we have a very good chance of making them think we are going for Sicily - it is an obvious target and should be nervous. On the other hand, they felt there was little hope of convincing the Boche that the extensive preparations in the eastern Mediterranean were also directed at Sicily. That is why they told Wilson that his cover plan should be something closer to the point, e.g. the Dodecanese. Since our relations with Turkey are now so obviously closer, the Italians must be rather worried about these islands.

I imagine you will agree with these arguments. I know that you will have your hands full at the moment and have not had much opportunity to discuss future operations with Eisenhower. But if by any chance you want to support Wilson's proposal, I hope you will let us know soon, because we cannot put it off any longer.

I am very sorry that we could not fulfil your wishes about the new commander of the Brigade Guards. Your own candidate has been hit by a bad bout of influenza and will probably not really give up for a few more weeks. No doubt, however, you know Forster personally; he did very well commanding a brigade back home and is, I believe, the best comrade available.

You must be as fed up as we are with the whole issue of war medals and Purple Hearts. We all agree with you that we do not want to offend our American friends, but there is more to it than that. If our troops serving in a particular theatre were to get extra decorations simply because Americans also serve there, we would face a good deal of discontent among those troops fighting elsewhere perhaps just as bitterly - or more so. My feeling is that we should thank the Americans for their kind offer, but say firmly that it would cause too many anomalies and we regret not being able to accept it. But it is on the agenda for the next military members' meeting and I hope you will make a decision soon.

Good luck
Yours always,
Archie Nye

SUPERMARINA

INCOMING MESSAGE

No. 19059

May 1943 - 0040 hours

Reserved Personnel

Transmitter: GERMAN TRAFFIC BROADCASTING OFFICE AT SUPERMARINA
German Navy High Command (OKM) 1 SKL reports 215509 the following:

Reserved for the person

K O in Spain reports that an English courier has been grounded in Spain. He was carrying a personal letter from the Chief of the Imperial General Staff addressed to General Alexander dated 23 April.

1)   Two landing companies are planned, named HUSKY et BRIMSTONE.

2)   HUSKY probably means Greece. In any case, it is planned to reinforce the 5^a Division to attack Cape ARAXS and the 56^a Division to attack Calamata.

3)   3rd BRIMSTONE probably means an enterprise in the western Mediterranean.

4)   A dummy enterprise on the Dodecanese and a dummy enterprise on Sicily are proposed for the HUSKY enterprise and for the BRIMSTONE enterprise.

5)   K O in Spain will send copies of the originals.

German Traffic Protection Office

S.I.S. Uff/B

Draft letter completed around 9-10 May 1943 SUPERMARINA
[draft letter not sent].

Prot. No. XXX   XXX, on ....

Personal Confidentiality

ARGUMENT : *Operational intentions of the enemy.*

SUPREME COMMAND - P.M. 21

1) The three enclosed pieces of information are particularly reliable.

2) The first (Annex 1) and the second (Annex 2) agree that landing operations in the Western Mediterranean are imminent and exclude that they are directed against the coasts and islands of Spain.
This leaves the coast of Provence, Sardinia and Sicily as likely targets.
The intensification of air actions over the Sicilian ports, the advantages of conquering the positions in Tunisia, and the possibility of gaining control of the Sicilian Channel through the possession of western Sicily would lead to the conclusion that this was the operation the enemy would attempt first.
However, the current deployment of landing craft is better prepared for an attack on Sardinia.
As long as this deployment is not modified and as long as work is not carried out to make Tunisia's naval and air positions even partially effective (dredging - even partial opening of the ports and airports), it must be assumed that the enemy's first objective is Sardinia and that any actions against Sicily (such as the air actions of 8-9 May) are a feint or have other contingent purposes (to make it difficult for our forces concentrated on the Capo Bon peninsula to be refuelled and protected by air).

3) This appreciation is confirmed in the third information (Annex 3).

This foresees two landing operations, one in the Western Mediterranean, with a feint towards Sicily and an unspecified main target, but which it seems logical to assume is Sardinia, and one in the Eastern Mediterranean that would include a feint against the Dodecanese and an actual action against the Morea wing aimed at occupying the airfields of Araxos and Calamata.

These clarifications make the information particularly reliable.
The operation in the Eastern Mediterranean directed against the weakest area of our deployment for the conquest of targets of primary importance for subsequent air operations is highly probable.
However, a prior concentration of naval transport and convoy escort units in the Levant is necessary for such an operation. The outflow of such units through the Sicilian Channel will take some time and, in any case, should not go unnoticed.

4) In conclusion, in the current state of affairs, an operation directed at the occupation of Sardinia must be assumed imminent; operations towards other objectives are less likely.

THE CHIEF OF STAFF

Annotation: *Acts.*

Annex n. 1

ROYAL NAVY STAFF

9 May 1943-XXI

No. 33877 - Germanic Fiduciary Source (9/5/43) communicates:

An Anglo-American landing operation targeting southern France aut the Tyrrhenian islands is believed to be imminent (even at the end of the week).

Annex n. 2

ROYAL NAVY STAFF

9 May 1943-XXI

No. 33875 -   Particularly reliable source reports that Admiral Gibraltar in conversation with Spanish officer hinted that east landing a matter of days (halt) It is strongly believed that operations against territories aut Spanish islands should be ruled out

Annex n. 3

GERMAN TRAFFIC PROTECTION OFFICE

No. 1905 - German Navy High Command (OKM) 1 SKL reports 215509 the following

Reserved Personnel

K O in Spain reports that an English courier has been grounded in Spain. He was carrying a personal letter from the Chief of the Imperial General Staff addressed to General Alexander dated 23 April.

1)   Two landing companies are planned, named HUSKY et BRIMSTONE.

2)   HUSKY probably means Greece. In any case, it is planned to reinforce the 5^a Division to attack Cape ARAXS and the 56^a Division to attack Calamata.

3) BRIMSTONE probably means an enterprise in the western Mediterranean.

4)A dummy enterprise on the Dodecanese and a dummy enterprise on Sicily are proposed for the HUSKY enterprise and for the BRIMSTONE enterprise.

5) K O in Spain will send copies of the originals.

MILITARY ATTACHÉ OFFICE BERLIN

DEPARTING TELEGRAM

For encrypted teletype

Addressed to Supreme Command

Berlin, 14 May 1943 at 09.50 hrs.

(*Text*)

Prot. no. 765/S alt *Pope*

I transmit the following reply of the Führer to Teletype 12959/Op dated 13 current alt: Start text reply alt

"Duce. In the telegraphic possession received today through your General at my O.K.W. I am with you in the conviction that the defence of the Italian islands is now in the foreground. I also agree with you that first of all the appropriate means of defence must be provided, including supplies for a long fight. In this respect, I can refer to the German supply of artillery, anti-tank guns and ammunition as well as my continuous insistence, most recently with the dispatch of the Grand Admiral, on the timely provision of the necessary supplies to the islands. As for sending German troops, I have no intention of sending five divisions. Rather, taking into account my own situation, I have limited myself to asking for your consent for the "Hermann Göring" division to be gathered and completed around the nuclei already in Italy and for the transport of the first parachute division to be considered. As a third of the divisions that you consider sufficient, the German units currently employed on the Italian islands could be worthwhile, which in Sicily, considered according to their numerical strength and not their fighting efficiency, constitute two weak regiments comma and in Sardinia little more than a reinforced battalion. To these must be added the German units which, with your consent, are currently being formed in southern Italy from the contingents that were destined for Tunisia and which should primarily serve as a gradual reinforcement of the German combat groups stationed on the islands. Almost all of these units are improvised with remnants of wards, marching battalions and soldiers on leave and returned from health resorts. For their prompt organisation and effective training, I have therefore also provided for a German army corps command, which will also be at your disposal for tactical deployment if necessary. In addition to this, German troops of a maximum effective strength of three divisions in total are planned by me to reinforce the defence of Italy and the islands, which, however, can only be deployed on the islands gradually in accordance with the supply situation. The only German forces that are currently in Italy, and which in total are much smaller than the strength of a division, have so far been indicated as three divisions, which has only been done to mislead the enemy, and for this reason it would be inadvisable to maintain this indication. My orders to equip the divisions in Sicily and Sardinia with tank units have already been given. In this regard, please consider that a successful deployment of these tank battalions also requires a corresponding framing of German troops, and is conditioned by command, training and armament units. In accordance with your wishes, I have also arranged for the necessary supplies to be brought to Corsica so that a tank battalion can be deployed there in the near future within the framework of approximately one reinforced regiment, which would also be taken from the three divisions. The German troops in Italy will be placed territorially and, as soon as they are ready for deployment, also tactically under the command of the competent Italian commands; as also corresponds to my wishes the assumption of the Führungabteiilung of the O.B.S. by the Southern Command itself. As liaison officer between the O.B.S. and the General Staff of the Italian Army, General von Rintelen is at your disposal. I beg you Duce to issue the necessary orders as soon as possible so that the transports can proceed without delay.

As far as the aviation situation is concerned, the departments currently in Italy are sufficiently well staffed. Only fighter aircraft are lacking. In addition to this, a further 200 fighters will be supplied in May. With this, the second air fleet will be reinforced in fighter aircraft for a strength of approximately 34 squadrons. In addition, four Italian fighter squadrons are currently being converted to German model aircraft. As far as combat formations are concerned, there are currently 9 squadrons, of which 60 aircraft and crews have already arrived ready for deployment. In addition, a further 6 squadrons will be launched in May and a further 3 squadrons in June. With the influx of 18 combat squadrons, your request is almost fulfilled. In addition, two squadrons of Italian Stukas are being converted to German material alt The following anti-aircraft artillery is currently being shipped: 71 pieces of

88 mm, 18 37 mm pieces, 30 20 mm pieces, 27 quadruple machine guns. A total of 18 heavy and 6 light batteries. Within 10 days, 48 88 mm pieces will still be flowing, which equals 12 heavy batteries. Even if these 30 heavy batteries do not yet completely satisfy your request, an attempt will be made to follow up the missing batteries as soon as possible.

Like first remedy
There please of provide travel from northern Italy.

Please accept Duce my warmest regards. Signed Adolf Hitler.

It ends.
O.K.W. please communicate now presentation to the Duce this teletype.
General Marras.

APPOINTMENTS

RELATING TO THE COLLOQUIUM HELD AT PALAZZO VENEZIA ON 17 MAY 1943-XXI

5 specimens - 1ˢᵗ copy

Present:

DUCE

His Excellency Army General AMBROSIO

Field Marshal KESSELRING

General von RINTELEN

Mar Kesselring - During my recent stay in Sicily, I had the opportunity to see the German troops and to examine their future task. With regard to German-Italian collaboration, I had contacts with Ecc. Roatta and General Monti. All the various problems were taken into consideration.

Duce - What is the general situation.

Mar. Kesselring - Forces are still lacking. I promised Ecc. Roatta that I would do everything in my power.

Duce - At what point is the organisation of the German troops?

Mar. Kesselring - The available forces correspond to two regiments and a third. Part of the artillery is still missing. In 10 or 14 days at most, the division will be completely in place (one regiment in Trapani, one in Palermo, these are strong regimental nuclei).

Duce - And tanks?

Mar. Kesselring - We currently have 56 of them, who were supposed to go to Tunisia and have been detained. They already form an organic department. Ecc. Roatta was of the idea of gathering them together in the middle of the island. I advised against it, pointing out that the 'Tiger' is very powerful, but its speed is limited. Instead, I would propose the relocation of part of these tanks to the east and part to the west.

I also looked at everything concerning passive defence, mainly what relates to airfields. They are very close to the coast and so there are two solutions: either secure their defence or destroy them.

Duce - The centre of Sicily is hilly and does not lend itself to landing fields. It is therefore necessary to defend those we have.

Mar. Kesselring - Anti-aircraft batteries, which are also anti-tank, offer a fairly good defence capability. They can also be used for anti-landing defence. These batteries, as you can see, have multiple tasks and form a robust complex. The defence of the camps will be supplemented with mines.

10,000 are already in Italy, another 120,000 are on the way.

Etc. Ambrosio - Sardinia also lacks mines.

Mar. Kesselring - Yes, but these 120,000 and then some wire arrive. But of course there is no possibility of defending oneself solely behind minefields and wire. You have to work day by day, feverishly.

Recent aerial photographs show that the concentration of naval forces in the port of Djidjelli has increased somewhat, yesterday it was no longer possible to provide, otherwise I would have suspended the bombing action on Bona and chosen this target. An attack in force is already planned for this evening.

Ecc. Roatta says that in two or three months the whole organisation should be in place (building of strongholds).

Duce - I am of the opinion that the main attack will come from Malta and not Tunisia.

Mar. Kesselring - As far as Malta is concerned, from what I have gathered from aerial photographs, the naval forces stationed there are not such as to suggest an action against Sicily. Only one ship of those present lends itself to the transport of troops for a landing, all the others are warships.

Etc. Ambrosio - I believe that a landing would be attempted at the extremes and not in the centre.

Mar. Kesselring - At present, the British do not have the necessary availability of aircraft carriers, whereas Tunisia and Malta have the possibility of covering possible actions with fighter aviation. This possibility should be considered.

Etc. Ambrosio - I consider it more likely that air actions will be carried out over Italy, some landing actions at the extremes of the island.

Duce - In such cases it is always best to consider the worst-case scenario.

Mar. Kesselring - Given the large amount of material in Djidjelli, the situation must be constantly monitored.

Duce - I have heard of your imminent departure!

Mar. Kesselring - I was summoned by the Fuehrer to his Headquarters and therefore felt it was my duty to present myself to you.

Duce - Tell the Fuehrer that I have written to him. The main subject is always that of defence (tanks, anti-aircraft and counter-tank weapons). I believe that with three German organic divisions, we can be safe for Italy, Sicily and Sardinia.

Etc. Ambrosio - (I have heard that it is the intention to increase the number of battalions in Sicily and Sardinia. However, I believe that these forces still scattered throughout Italy need to be reunited).

Duce - They were to be three organic divisions, however, with tanks, anti-aircraft artillery and counter-tank artillery. Since October, he has foreseen a tightening of air actions over the entire Italian territory. The need for defence against such actions is therefore apparent. The population is calm, but there is always the problem of the population's lives. If it sees that the passive defence is good, it is calm. (Mention the action du Civitavecchia).

Mar. Kesselring - Even before the end of the Tunisian campaign, I had already given the order that the entire air force was to be moved. The Flak was increased. However, given the high altitude at which the Anglo-American aircraft operate, it is difficult to hit them.

What, then, is the subject of your writing, Duce, to the Fuehrer?

Duce - Defence against air actions over territory in the foreground. Also defence by means of fighter planes.

The population sees that attacks are more and more frequent, while the aircraft shot down are few (e.g. at Cagliati: out of 400 raiding aircraft, 4 or 5 are shot down by us).

Mar. Kesselring - But they were less than 400.

As far as hunting is concerned, a transformation in its use has become necessary. This transformation is in progress.

Duce - I understand, always when you change the system, you go through a period of crisis.

Mar. Kesselring - As for the use of a division in Sicily, half of which was located in the east and half in the west

Duce - This we shall see in the future.

Mar. Kesselring - (Representing the possible difficulty of transporting a complete division by rail, considering the enormous amount of material currently being transported).

Etc. Ambrosio - But the 'H. Goering" and the paratroopers must come. We're sending the parachutists to Livorno, for later deployment in Sardinia. The "H. Goering" will be launched in Sicily. Then there's the third division formed by the elements that will gather in Italy

Mar. Kesselring - I understand that the 'H. Goering" was to gather in the Naples area.

Etc. Ambrosio - No, there's too much stuff in Naples, we arranged for it to meet in Calabria. Perhaps the Field Marshal is not yet aware of this, because he arranged it only this morning. precisely

Etc. von Rintelen (takes note).

R. AIR FORCE GENERAL STAFF

Operations Office   Military Mail 3300, 1 July 1943-XXI

Prot. N. 1B/10506

Secret

SUBJECT: *Appreciation of the situation.*

        TO COMMAND 1a AIR SQUADRON

        TO COMMAND 2a AIR SQUADRON

        TO COMMAND 3a AIR SQUADRON

        TO COMMAND 4a AIR SQUADRON

        TO COMMAND AERONAUTICA SICILIA

        TO THE SARDINIA AIR FORCE COMMAND

For your information and regulation, the following appreciation of the situation is transmitted:

Many symptoms suggest that the enemy has completed its preparation and is about to begin the new operational cycle. The following appreciation can be made of the probable objectives and mode of action:

    1.   –   It must be assumed that the enemy will operate in areas where they can *benefit from maximum air support.*

From this point of view, taking into account the air deployment that, according to the information in our possession, the enemy would have assumed and the possibilities offered by the fields of Malta and Pantelleria, south-eastern Sicily (from Syracuse to Gela), south-western Sicily (from Gela to Trapani) and, to a lesser extent, southern Sardinia (Gulf of Cagliari) are considered particularly exposed.

2.   – The forces that the enemy will have to embark on will be significant and will involve a large number of landing craft.

Furthermore, if, as is probable, the enemy intends to avoid a strong direct confrontation by exploiting periods of crisis in defence caused by intense local aerial bombardment, the landing will have to be executed very quickly.

It will then have to *choose an area that includes a port* on which to initially concentrate air attacks and then launch the majority of the means for a very rapid landing *to be carried out during the day.*

Taking into account local defences and hydrographical conditions, the probability ranking of the enemy targets examined above can be adjusted as follows:

1°) Trapani – Sciacca

2°) Cagliari – S.Antioco

3°) Siracusa.

3.   – However, the enemy's deployment of landing craft still has its centre of gravity far to the west.

Even taking into account movements that may be executed at the last moment, it must be assumed that there is an *equal probability that the enemy offence will be directed* against *Sardinia or Sicily.*

4.   – The last element to be considered is the considerable reinforcement of the British Mediterranean Battle F.N. that counts today:

- 6 battleships

- 3 aircraft carriers

- around 20 cruisers

- 60 or so destroyers

In conclusion, the reinforcement of the British Mediterranean fleet is evidently an indication that *enemy preparedness is virtually complete,* although it does not provide any new elements to further specify towards which area the enemy effort will be directed.

p. THE CHIEF OF STAFF

F/to Santoro

SUPERMARINA

Personal Confidentiality

NOTICE

N. progressivo 9869 data 4 Luglio 1943-XXI

Serial No. 9869 dated 4 July 1943-XXI

RECIPIENT:

SUPREME COMMAND

and, for information: SUPERAEROE SUPERESERCYTE

CAPO SCORTE 2ª FLOTTA AEREA at Supermarina for O.B.S.

The following appreciation of the situation formulated by the Strategic Reconnaissance Committee at 180004 is transmitted.

- Slightly worsening sea. Bad visibility especially along the N.A.F. coasts.

- The deployment of air forces was examined on reports from

O.B.S. and by Superaereo. The numerical evaluations agree for the western sector; they differ significantly for the eastern sector for which Superaereo believes there are greater forces than those listed by O.B.S.

Furthermore, Superaereo estimates a higher percentage of aircraft normally ready for deployment. In any case, this is an important deployment that, for the Algerian-Tunisian sector, certainly allows strong air support for offensive operations against our major islands, especially Sicily.

In the eastern sector, for now, the air force would not seem to be sufficient to support a very important operation.

No reports of changes in the deployment of landing craft.

There is no information on the location of battleships and aircraft carriers other than those already reported.

The naval deployment, including two support groups in French North African waters, is already sufficient, as is the air force, to begin operations.

However, there is no indication of an immediate start.

RICCARDI

SUPERMARINE MESSAGE

TRANSMITTED TO THE RECIPIENT COMMANDS AT 1930 HOURS ON 7 JULY 1943-XXI

LITTORIO PER F.N.B.	per telearmonica [telefono segreto]
MARINA LA SPEZIA	telearmonica
MARINA NAPOLI	telearmonica
MARINA TARANTO	telearmonica
MARI PROVENZA	telearmonica
MARI CORSICA	posta
MARINA LA MADDALENA	telearmonica
MARINA MESSINA	posta
MARIMOREA	posta

Strictly Confidential to the Person

Supermarina .... alt For your personal guidance we convey the following appreciation of the current situation.

(First) Considering as a unit of measurement the total number of means required to transport a reinforced infantry division, the landing craft currently deployed in North Africa are estimated as follows: ports west of Bizerte two; Bizerte and Tunis three and a half; Susa half; Sfax one; Tripoli one.

(Second) The land forces, including specially trained divisions for landings, airborne divisions and paratroopers are also in most cases assembled in Tunisia.

(Third) There is a lack of reliable information on the air deployment, which is certainly impressive; however, there are more than 400 aircraft, especially fighters on the fields of Malta, about 1900 fighters and 1150 bombers in French North Africa and about 190 four-engine aircraft in the Benghazi area.

(Four) The six British battleships now present in the Mediterranean, the two aircraft carriers and the two recently arrived monitors, have left Gibraltar, and it has not yet been possible to ascertain their whereabouts; however, it is believed that no major unit has sailed to the east of Cape Bon.

(Fifth) From day four, systematic air action was begun against airports in Sicily alt Action was progressively intensified and also extended to ports Trapani - Porto Empedocle - Licata.

(Sixth) It is believed that the enemy is ready to begin landing operations in Sicily and possibly with diversionary character in Sardinia. Commencement of such operations depends on conducting air preparatory phase whose duration is not foreseeable but could be very short - 1830007.

Ernest ZOLLING

Staff Colonel

Former Chief Information Officer of the OBS.

Neustadt, 29 October 1947

SITUATION OF THE ENEMY BEFORE LANDING IN SICILY

After the enemy had broken the German-Italian resistance in North Africa in May 1943, it was clear to the OBS that the enemy would in every way try to exploit the result achieved. Seen as a whole, the Allied victory in North Africa, which had completely eliminated the enemy in that area, could only be one part of a development operation. The Allies had succeeded in dealing a severe blow to the German-Italian alliance through the destruction of the Army of Africa, depriving it of valiant fighters and extremely important material.

But the most important part of the success was the conquest of a large base and attack bases against southern Europe. The advantage of possessing such bases was all the more sensitive because of the Axis maritime and air inferiority in the Mediterranean, which took away those bases and attack possibilities. Apart from unimportant disturbances, the march of the Allied forces by land, sea and air could take place according to the established plans.

After realising that the Tunisian victory had not been followed by an immediate attack against Italy, the OBS was convinced that the Allies would take their time before commencing further operations.

The Allied units that the battle had brought into Tunisian territory, both the Anglo-American ones from the west and those of the attacking 8ᵃ [British] Army from the east, needed a long time to be reorganised and prepared for the new action.

It was also to be assumed that they would be subjected to special instruction for landing operations.

It was also likely that, to lessen the risk factor, additional forces would be sent from the United States and the British Empire. In the same way, the air operations against our airfields and communications backwaters, linked to the landing operation, also took some time. For all these reasons, the OBS did not consider a major attack likely before mid-June 1943. After that time, however, the start of the operation was considered possible.

The Allied forces that were deployed in North Africa towards the end of the fighting in Tunisia were generally known to the German Command, both from the contacts they had had during the action and from the efficiency of the Information Service that had remained in operation in North Africa.

Aerial reconnaissance, which continued to function despite all the difficulties encountered, also brought results.

Gradually the news about the Allied forces in North Africa became more and more exact and precise. Overall, the Allies had some 20-25 divisions ready for combat; in addition, there were all those army troops with which the security of the Mediterranean countries - including Egypt and the Middle East - was guaranteed.

Even if it did not appear that all landing craft were available to bring all those troops in one wave, their ready deployment in the combat zone with a commuter system of transport was always considered possible.

In order to judge the Allied readiness for the planned landing operation, it was very important to continuously monitor how many 'Task Force' divisions had landing craft available.

At the beginning of July 1943, landing craft were available for the transport of about 12 divisions. Of course, these landing craft could be supplemented by transports by normal ships if needed.

According to reports, the bulk of the allied forces in mid-June were in Tunisia and Algeria.

Subsequent reports of continuous transfers of forces to Tunisia, as well as the existing massing there, suggested that Tunisia would be the main launching pad for the landings.

It was to be assumed that the landing forces would in principle consist of Anglo-American divisions only, as the French divisions were not yet sufficiently equipped and trained. It was also to be assumed that the American and British divisions, although under the single command of General Eisenhower, would operate grouped in an American army and a British parmata, for matters of command, employment and supplies.

However, it was not made clear that he would take over command of the British units involved in the landing, as command of the 1ª and the 8ª Army was available.

Through the radio interception service, the OKW was convinced that at the end of the fighting in Tunisia, the 8thª Army had been transferred to the Middle East.

As the OBS was of an absolutely contrary opinion, there were strong disagreements at that time between the OKW and the OBS about the fate of the 8ª Army. The OBS was only aware of the transfer of the 2ª New Zealand Division to Egypt-Palestine, while, from the reports in its possession, it appeared that the other units of the 8ª Army had remained in the Tunisian and Tripoline area.

Although the location of the Allied troops was known, at least from a general point of view, one could not venture any predictions as to how the enemy would conduct the war. The Allied Intelligence Service managed to disguise its plans very well at that time. This was achieved not by maintaining absolute secrecy, but instead by propagating a large number of reports about probable landing operations that reached the German Command through various sources, some of which contradicted each other and some of which were confirmed. It was difficult in the large number of reports received to distinguish the probable from the true. Spain, southern France, Italy and Greece were repeatedly mentioned as landing targets. A special report of absolute confidence received in mid-May spoke of Sardinia and the Peloponnese [Operation 'Mincemeat']. Even the concentration of Allied forces in the centre of the North African coastline did not in itself provide a valid and reliable indication for predicting the Allied Command's decisions. Ultimately, the Algerian and Tunisian ports were the only ports available in the western and central Mediterranean from which any landing operations against the southern European coasts could be launched.

The OBS considered the landing in the area where it exercised its command, namely 'in the Apennine peninsula and adjacent islands', to be likely. This conviction was reinforced by concomitant reports of agents and in mid-June by the conquest of the islands of Pantelleria and Lampedusa (which, however, could be interpreted as a masking action) as well as by the increasingly violent and numerous air attacks by the Allies against the Axis Air Force installations and against the lines of connection and traffic in the Italian area.

From the methodical and systematic attacks, which had caused a paralysis of traffic and the Axis Air Force, it was possible to recognise that the decisive blow of the Landing Army was about to be struck.

When in the second half of June the approach of the landing became more and more evident, it was of decisive importance for the German Command to be able to establish the exact time and place of the landing.

All available means were employed for this purpose: aerial reconnaissance, radiotelegraphic interception, submarine exploration and the intelligence service. But the countermeasures of the Allied intelligence service considerably reduced our chances. Aerial reconnaissance was only rarely able to pass through enemy fighter aircraft: against our radiotelegraphic interception the enemy opposed radiotelegraphic silence, submarines were kept away from the enemy's anti-som fighters and news of agents in North Africa became increasingly scarce. Only a few reports of trusted agents, and almost always late, reached the German Command. Instead, the continued observation of the Strait of Gibraltar proved to be a safe mean of exploration. The traffic through the strait, especially with regard to ship types, allowed important and safe deductions about Allied plans.

Inoltre l'ingresso in Mediterraneo di navi da battaglia, specialmente delle corazzate inglesi a fine giugno – primi luglio 1943, era un chiaro segno che lo sbarco era imminente. L'arrivo al principio di luglio di diverse navi ospedali a breve distanza l'una dall'altra accentuava l'imminenza dell'azione. Le suppletive informazioni degli agenti in Tunisia e Algeria relativa a movimenti di truppa per via terrestre e marittima da ovest verso est avvalorarono decisamente le previsioni di un attacco a brevissima scadenza. Qualche notizia al principio di luglio indicava che nei porti tunisini erano in corso operazioni di imbarco. L'interpretazione di tutte le notizie di cui disponeva convinsero l'OBS che dal principio del mese di luglio lo sbarco poteva essere atteso da un giorno all'altro.

Moreover, the entry of battleships, especially British battleships into the Mediterranean in late June - early July 1943, was a clear sign that the landing was imminent. The arrival in early July of several hospital ships within a short distance of each other accentuated the imminence of action. Supplementary information from agents in Tunisia and Algeria concerning troop movements by land and sea from west to east decisively corroborated the predictions of a very short-term attack. A few reports in early July indicated that embarkation operations were underway in Tunisian ports. The interpretation of all the news at its disposal convinced the OBS that from the beginning of July the landing could be expected any day now.

While little doubt could remain as to the time of the landing, nothing was known of the location of the landing. There was no certain news about it and it can be said that there was none until the enemy landing fleet was sighted. The German Command could only rely on signs and indirect indications.

To these belonged the strong attacks carried out in early July by the Allied Air Force on airports, traffic points and military targets (troop concentrations, fortifications, supply depots, etc.) in Sicily, Calabria, Apulia.

Since almost the entirety of the allied air forces in the Mediterranean were employed for attacks in those areas, it could almost certainly be concluded that they would be the first target of the invading army.

One could not be sure whether the attack on Sicily was an end in itself, or whether instead the conquest of the island was considered by the Allied Command from the point of view of gaining a launching point for a subsequent and almost simultaneous attack on the southern part of the Italian peninsula.

The consequence was to also deploy part of the available German reserves in Sicily, to try to provide our ally with at least some support.

To the German Command, one point appeared clear and beyond dispute: Italy, after the defeat in Africa and having suffered the Allied air attacks aimed at destroying nerves and cities, attacks that consequently facilitated the work of enemy propaganda, could no longer offer decisive resistance.

The Italian people and army in the summer of 1943 were tired of the war and in any case convinced in their hearts that it was now impossible to achieve a decision of the war by force of arms.

So in the first ten days of July, the German High Command was full of concern about the situation that would arise in southern Italy. By now the lightning bolt of an Allied landing could strike the old cradles of Mediterranean culture and open a new war front on European soil.

This situation of high tension and expectation came to an end on the afternoon of 9 July, when a reconnaissance aircraft reported sighting a convoy of several landing craft, heavily escorted by naval and air units, heading from Malta towards the southern tip of Sicily.

The first invasion of Europe had begun.

▲ Dozens of US Army M4 Sherman tanks wait to board LSTs in the port of La Pêcherie, Tunisia, two days before the start of Operation Husky, the landing in Sicily on 10 July 1943.

SUPERMARINA

SECRET   19 JULY 1943-XXI

SUMMARY OF PRAISE FOR ENEMY ACTION AGAINST SICILY

Preliminary remarks

Dai "Notiziari della guerra navale"

1° July: … in summary, it is appreciated that at the present time the deployment of enemy landing craft is directed mainly against Sicily and is such that it can be attacked at any time.

4 July: … there are no new noteworthy elements regarding the deployment of the landing craft, so the assessment of the past few days is still valid.

6 July: … the persistence of low clouds over the enemy ports has not [made it] possible to gather new elements regarding the deployment of enemy craft in the last few days. Only a photograph taken of Bizerte at 180005 showed that the situation of the landing craft was practically unchanged from that recorded on 29 June, but it was observed that the majority of the landing craft were either loaded or under load. In the final analysis, therefore, in the absence of more complete information and in view of the transfer of the heavy naval forces to the east, the assessment of the past few days is still valid: that is, it is believed that, given the enemy's deployment, an attack on Sicily could be attempted at any time.

7 July: … from the scanty information available, and considering the decisive air action recently undertaken by the enemy against the Sicilian airfields and against the ports in the western and southern parts of the island, it is believed that the enemy has already begun an operational cycle against Sicily. It is not possible to estimate how long the current preparatory phase will last, but it is noted that the enemy's deployment is such that it will be able to take action at any time.

8 July: … regarding sightings and reports of enemy units in the Licata-Gela area last night, it is noted that … the aforementioned area will be one of those chosen by the enemy for a landing attempt.

9 July: … no new reconnaissance of enemy ports nor anything of note, except for the sighting of a convoy of 70 to 90 units at 032009, south of Pantelleria, east route. It should be a landing party bound for Malta and almost certainly coming from Bizerte. If the sighting was confirmed, it should be interpreted as a further reinforcement of the landing force destined to act from Malta and would constitute an indication of a threat to the Licata - Syracuse area.

Preliminary sightings

-        On the afternoon of the 8th the II CAT by means of a reconnaissance on sight of Bizerte, from which it appeared that the port had practically emptied. This would have been a strong indication that an attack was imminent, but - when asked to confirm this - O.B.S. stated that the reconnaissance was absolutely unreliable.

-        No sightings of enemy convoy movements bound for Malta, except for the above-mentioned 032009, which was deemed to require confirmation, reached Supermarina until the evening of the 9th.

News, appreciations and dispositions at the time of action.

18.25 – Maricolleg Frascati communicates outcome of reconnaissance on Bizerte in the afternoon, from which the port appears almost empty. We ask for confirmation if the reconnaissance is complete and reliable

18.35 – Superaereo announces that CAT aircraft sighted at 16.30 five groups of units and landing craft on the north coast of Malta with route between NE and NW.

19.15 – Maricolleg Frascati confirms the above sighting.

19.30 – Supermarina orders German torpedo motorboats (Italian ones will not be able to leave Trapani because of bad weather) to leave Porto Empedocle towards Augusta. (The MS were then forced to fall back towards the west, off Licata, due to violent enemy reaction).

19.40 – Maricolleg Frascati reports news of the day's air actions against the airports of Sicily, the destruction of the Tactical Command of the II CAT and the relative interruption of communications.

21.30 – Maricolleg Frascati reports that at 1935 a convoy of 33 mg was sighted. From Gozo a convoy of 40 landing craft heading 350°, escorted by 4 probable battleships and 3 cruisers, followed by another one of about 45 units and 3 probable aircraft carriers.

22.25 – Maricolleg reports sighting of 18 probable landing craft, at 19.20 at 24 mg. for 50° from Pantelleria, route unspecified. And, at 6.10 pm, at 109 mg. for 120° from Malta, 2 battleships - one aircraft carrier - 4 cruisers - route 290°.

22.30 – Maricolleg reports sighting of about 15 - 20 unspecified units 30 mg. North of Gozo, northern route.

22.40 – Supermarina orders the immediate departure of 6 Submarines for the planned ambushes of Dina 12.

22.55 – Messina communicates information from Catania that Syracuse is in anti-ship action.

23.04 – Maricolleg reports that at 22.10 20 naval units with air escort have been sighted, about 15 mg. South of Capo Passero.

23.20 – Maricolleg reports that, according to II CAT, Syracuse is bombarded from the sea.

23.57 – Maricolleg informs that CAT aircraft at 19.27 sighted 26 mg.Per 210° from Galite a convoy of 21 steamers, 2 cruisers, route East.

10 JULY

00.05 – Maricolleg announces that at 23.50 paratroopers have been launched in the Comiso area.

00.25 - Supermarina confirms to LITTORIO for FNB [Forze Navali da Battagli], to stand by for ignition.

00.36 - Maricolleg announces that an enemy convoy is at 17 mg. For 220° from Licata course 340°.

00.50 hours - Marina Messina reports that there is fighting on land at Capo Passero.

00.53 hours-Maricolleg reports that at 24.00 paratroopers have been dropped at S. Pietro.

01.25 hours - Marina Messina reports that the C.FF.AA [Air Force Command]. of Sicily at 01.00 has given the state of emergency and the order to destroy the ports of Licata and Porto Empedocle.

The man
who never was

by EWEN MONTAGU

BIBLIOGRAPHY

Books

Crowdy, Terry, Deceiving Hitler: Double-Cross and Deception in World War II., Oxford, 2008, p. 195.

Deakin Frederick W., *Storia della Repubblica di Salò*, (traduzione di Renzo De Felice), Enaudi, Torino, 1963.

Eisenhower David Dwight, *Crociata in Europa* (dall'inglese *Crusade in Europe*), Arnoldo Mondadori, Milano, 1949

Kriegstagebuch der Seekriegsleitung/Operationsabteilung, parte A [KTB 1.Skl, A], Berlin-Bonn-Herford, Mittler & Sohn, 1988.

Liddell Hart B.H., *Storia Miliare della seconda Guerra mondiale* (dall'inglese *History of the Second World War*) , Mondadori, Milano, 1970

Liddell Hart B.H, *Storia di una sconfitta. Parlano i generali del III Reich*, Rizzoli, Milano, 1973 (3ª edizione)

Macintyre Ben, *Operation Mincemeat, The Nazis and Assured an Allied Victory*, Harmony Books, New York, 2010.

Mattesini Francesco, *La partecipazione tedesca alla Guerra aeronavale nel Mediterraneo (1940-1945)"* (coautore per la parte politica Alberto Santoni), Edizioni dell'Ateneo & Bizzarri, Roma, 1980 (2ª Edizione, Alberelli, Parma, 2005).

Mattesini Francesco (Cermelli Mario per correzione delle bozze), *Le direttive tecnico-operative di Superaereo*; Volume Secondo II Tomo, *Gennaio 1943 - Settembre 1943*, Stato Maggiore dell'Aeronautica Ufficio Storico, Roma, 1992.

Mattesini Francesco , *La Marina e l'8 settembre", I Tomo, "Le ultime operazioni offensive della Regia Marina e il dramma della Forza Navale da Battaglia"*; Ufficio Storico della Marina Militare, Roma, 2002.

Mattesini Francesco, *L'uomo che non è mai esistito*. In riferimento al film "L'uomo che non è mai esistito". L'operazione "Mincemeat" che non trasse in ingannò i Comandi dell'Asse in Italia, Roma, novembre 2021, nella pagina dell'Autore del sito academia edu.

Molony C.J.C & Flynt F.C. - Davies H.L. – Gleave T.P., *The Mediterranean and Middle East*, Volume V, HMSO, London, 1978.

Montegu Ewen, *The Man Who Never Was* (*L'uomo che non è mai esistito*), London Bloomsbury, 1953.

Mussolini Benito, *Storia di un anno. Il tempo del bastone e della Carota*, Mondadori, 1944-XXIII, p. 41-42.

Roskill S.W., "History of the Second World War United Kingdom Military Serie", *The Mediterranean and Middle East, The Campaign in Sicily and The Campaign in Italy 3rd September 1943 to 31st March 1944*, Volume III, Parte I, HMSO, London. Santoni Alberto *Le operazioni in Sicilia e in Calabria*, Stato Maggiore Esercito Ufficio Storico, Roma, 1989.

Salewski M., *Die deutsche Seekriegsleitung, 1935-1945*, Volume 111: DenkscIniften and Lagebtrachtungen 19, 38 – 1944, Bernard & Graefe, Frankfurt am Mein, 1973

Samuel Eliot Morison, *History of United States Naval Operations in World War II, Sicily – Salerno – Anzio, January 1943 – June 1944*, Castle Books, 2001.

Shepperd G.A., *La campagna d'Italia 1943-1945* (*The Italian Campaign 1943-1945*), Garzanti, Milano, 1970.

Smith Denis, *Deathly Deception*, Oxford University Press, 2010.

Von Senger und Etterlin Frido, (*Krieg in Europa*), *Combattere senza paura e senza speranza*. Longanesi, Milano, 1968.

WIKIPEDIA, *Operation Mincemeat*.

TITOLI GIÀ PUBBLICATI - TITLES ALREADY PUBLISHING

BOOKS TO COLLECT